THE
NAKED
WITCH

THE NAKED WITCH

FIONA HORNE

ROCKPOOL
PUBLISHING

A Rockpool book
PO Box 252
Summer Hill
NSW 2130
Australia
www.rockpoolpublishing.com.au
http://www.facebook.com/RockpoolPublishing

ISBN 9781925429633

First published in 2017
Copyright text © Fiona Horne 2017
Copyright design © Rockpool Publishing 2017
This edition published in 2017

National Library of Australia Cataloguing-in-Publication entry
Creator: Horne, Fiona, 1966- author.

Title: The naked witch / Fiona Horne.

9781925429633 (paperback)

Subjects: Horne, Fiona, 1966-
Witches—Australia—Biography.
Witchcraft—Australia.
Women television personalities—Australia—Biography.

Cover and internal design by Seymour Design
Typesetting by Graeme Jones
Printed and bound in Australia

Cover:
Photographer: Sasha Alexander
Assistant and Fire Safety: Michele Olson
Hair: Annie Barry Pendley
Interior Photo Editor Assistant: Alex Brown

Photos:
Cyrill Sipka: page 12, colour insert page 7; Tony Mott: page 64, colour insert page 4;
Andrew Rankin/Wildlight: page 99; Brett B.: page 156; RJB Images: page 170; Steve
Friedman: page 186; Sasha Alexander: pages 206, 215.

10 9 8 7 6 5 4 3 2 1

For the pirate from the pilot

CONTENTS

Prologue **9**

Introduction
THE NAKED WITCH **13**

YOU SHOULD HAVE BEEN
PUT IN A BUCKET **17**

A GIFTED BUT TROUBLED CHILD **35**

WE ARE SURFERS OF THE MIND **59**

THANK GOD YOU LOOK LIKE ME **79**

FIONA THE HOT WITCH **95**

HOLLYWOOD'S HOTTEST COUGAR **131**

THE BROKEN-HEART SYNDROME **155**

THIS WILL BE THE BEST THING THAT
HAS EVER HAPPENED TO YOU **169**

A PLANE IS MORE COMFORTABLE
THAN A BROOMSTICK **185**

50 DOES NOT SUCK **205**

MJEJANE

South Africa, February 2016

have just completed a grueling bush-flying course.

Not on a broomstick … in a single-engine Cessna 172 aeroplane with giant tundra tyres. I am about to take off on a flying safari of South Africa and Namibia. My dream to grow my skills as a bush pilot is fueled by my desire to offer humanitarian aid and relief to stricken communities unserved by airports and other conveniences. Or, in cases of disaster, I would be sufficiently skilled to fly in inhospitable regions, safely landing and departing on dirt strips, mountain plains and other challenging environments where aid is needed. In fact, I flew the bush plane to this lodge in a private game reserve (offered by wonderful new friends I met during the course). Navigating here was easy: there were no complicated sectionals and a myriad of communications with multiple air traffic control stations – I just followed the river through the middle of the valley to a small airstrip. So simple is life now.

Outside in the front yard I can see, literally, a wild, raw world of elephants, hippos and rhinos. It's extraordinary. All the dream seeds I planted near and far, recent and long ago, have yielded this bounty – I am living and, more profoundly, *experiencing*, my dream.

How did I get here?

It was not an act of Witchcraft.

But a Witch did act.

My friend and avowed Witch Christian Day says, 'Fiona Horne embodies the Magick of Do.'

I have learned some secret and very powerful magick. It wasn't taught to me from a Circle of Initiates. I didn't read it in a book.

I lived it, by losing everything and learning to ask for nothing when all was gone.

Learning instead of asking, to give. Instead of holding, to let go. To trust that somehow what I needed would appear. And then learning to accept that I did not need to know, and in fact, must not pursue, anything specific.

I only had to show up to life – willing, authentic, humble and ready to be of service. The 'secret Magick' I had discovered would take care of everything else.

It's been twenty years since my first published works *Witch: A Personal Journey* and *Witch: A Magickal Year* hit the shelves in Australia and, ultimately, were woven together for overseas release in 2001. *Witch: A Magickal Journey* was published in the USA that year. *Publisher's Weekly* called it 'THE Witchcraft Book of 2001'.

Back in the 90s I was a celebrity 'chip off the old block' of grunge and electronic rock. After a seven-year career fronting a chart-topping Australian band called Def FX, which abruptly and unceremoniously ended in 1997, I parlayed my performing energy into TV and radio … and writing books about Witchcraft, which created a small international sensation for the next decade.

I can now describe myself as a professional pilot, fire dancer and yogini. I live on a small Caribbean island. I am active in youth outreach work and humanitarian-aid efforts.

And I am a Witch writing my autobiography as I look at an alligator resting on the riverbank and a warthog snuffling around in the grass. It occurs to me, does it matter that a Witch is writing this book? Perhaps no more than it would if a beloved Shaman like Don Miguel Ruiz, a Jewish Buddhist like conservative news anchorman Dan Harris, or some other established, culturally and intellectually acceptable mystic was behind the page.

So I say to Witches: no doubt you will recognise some of this journey and these trials.

And to non-Witches: no doubt you will recognise and relate to a lot of what I'm sharing, too.

My offerings are what has worked, and continues to work, for me.

They are what brought me here.

INTRODUCTION

The term, 'Naked Witch' conjures a number of different images: a Witch surrounded by flames (I do that intentionally when I firedance clothed or naked, depending on the audience), a 'skyclad' or 'clad by the sky' Witch in a ritual Coven gathered under a full moon (I have been that Witch a number of times), and spread-eagled across a double-page in Playboy (yes, I've done that too – twice).

'Naked Witch' could also be interpreted as a Witch with nothing to hide behind: no masks, no gothic make-up, no stereotypes; just a conscious, authentic creature – magickal and completely true. It is in this spirit that I call this book The Naked Witch.

After Googling me, a new friend said, 'So, Fiona, you're not like other celebrities who were famous – they don't tend to bounce back and be so completely different like you have done.'

And we had a discussion about people we know in the public eye (and some I know personally), whose lives are rooted firmly in a past that they perceive was better.

Despite so many difficult and disappointing events throughout my life, there's one rule that I embrace: If I'm going to keep living, I have to make the best of it.

I left Hollywood, and all the shallow and superficial things it upholds, not least because I did not want to be sixty and having plastic surgery in an attempt to look thirty. I'd rather be fifty and looking 'younger' naturally because I'm happy and doing something constructive and useful with my life.

So this book is about how I totally recreated my life to be something I can live and truly enjoy – through all its twists, turns and straight, wide-open roads. No compromises, no dumbing down, no people-pleasing.

Writing this book was often very hard. As I trawled through memories for the early chapters I just wanted to jump in the ocean and forget everything but this present moment.

In fact, I did just that. I took up freediving while writing this book and clocked my deepest freedive to date – 81 feet – on the home stretch of the first draft. As I wrote, the peace and inner stillness to be found on a single breath deep under the ocean became essential therapy.

I don't want this book to be just a drawn-out diatribe of my life. I want it to be useful and helpful to the people who read it. And I want it to be entertaining and enjoyable, otherwise why write it? I'm not financially motivated; I have learned to live with very little money, so having more would make little difference. I do have great wealth in the realms of experience and friendships. These are the assets I am motivated to cultivate.

I like who I am now; I didn't like who I was before.

As I've struggled with writing parts of this book I've considered that maybe the way this book can help me (as well as its readers) is by teaching me once and for all to have compassion for all my mistakes, insincerities, inauthenticity and embarrassments;

to forgive myself for not getting a grip on living in the moment sooner. I've been told I'm too hard on myself – but that's how I was taught to be.

So often I've wanted to call my publisher and say, 'Can we *not* do this? I don't want to resurrect the person I was.' But I pressed on. Because that's the one thing, through all the failures in my life, I've learned to do really well:

Not give up.

I hope my story is useful to you and that some of my lessons and thinking can help you conjure up lots of gratitude, fulfilment and serenity, too.

chapter one

YOU SHOULD HAVE BEEN PUT IN A BUCKET

'When you can't see the light at the end of the tunnel, you must crawl through it and light the bloody thing yourself.'

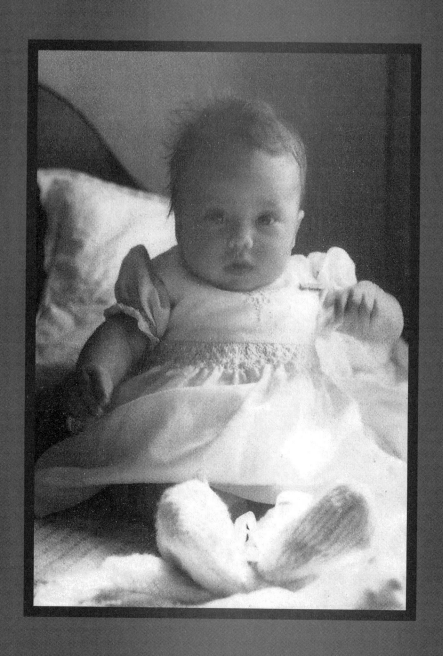

always knew I was adopted … I grew up feeling isolated and misunderstood – a rebel without understanding the cause, but knowing there was one – as I relentlessly searched for something different because I did not fit into where I was. My mother told me: 'You weren't an accident, we wanted you, we had to work hard to get you.' But, as it turned out, they were ultimately disappointed with what they got.

I had a hard time fitting in. My mother once told me that on my fifth birthday party, attended by some neighbourhood kids, she couldn't find me anywhere. Eventually she did – I was hiding in my wardrobe, reading a book. The kids picked on me and so I hid from them. Nowadays you'd call it bullying. Back then it was just normal.

I was a voracious reader from a young age. The books I really loved told stories about brave girls in faraway places. I tried running away a few times but I never got further than the end of the long dirt track that we lived on. It wasn't until I was fifteen that I really got away.

When I think back to that time in my life, I feel an uncomfortable twisting feeling in my stomach. My parents didn't like me; I was shunned by classmates; when I did make the cut and I was allowed into a circle of friends, I spent my whole time desperately appealing for their approval. So they had no respect for me.

I remember swimming in a school carnival race. I hated sports events; I hated being in the spotlight. I was always being accused of being 'up myself', anyway, and I'd grovel and say, 'No, I'm not. I hate myself.' I said that so often throughout my childhood that it became an anthem during my teens and adulthood – and I really have spent the last 30 years working to erase that statement from my brain. I finally banished it about five years ago when I was 45.

Back to the swimming race …

It was the 50-metre breaststroke, and I dived in and started to swim. I just did it – I didn't think about winning, only that I had to do this. After what seemed a long time I heard my mother's voice: 'Come on, Fiona. Come on, Fiona!' I looked up and saw her running along the side of the pool and calling out to me. I glanced behind me and saw, in the lane next to me, the best swimmer in my class (whose name was Carolyn) and … I was beating her! I looked to my left and realised I was beating everyone. The end of the pool was only a few metres away – I was going to win!

And so I slowed down and let Carolyn win.

After all, she was the better swimmer.

I remember getting to the end of the pool and not being able to lift myself out. My arms had never felt so weak.

People were yelling at me to get out. The next race was starting. I think my mother pulled me out of the pool.

I had come second.

Good – but not good enough. I'd made sure of that.

The kids at school called me 'Fish Lips' but this nickname had nothing to do with being in the pool that day. My classmates on the school bus ride, which was an hour each way from my home and which I was forced to endure, had given it to me. I have full lips. This was before they became trendy. Sometimes I am bewildered at the way women inject substances into their lips to fill them out when I was so scorned for them, growing up. 'Small tits, massive lips, Mrs Fish, Fiona Horne', was how the song went. There were other verses, and when I got on the bus every day there would be a rousing chorus. I spent my years from age 10–15 covering my mouth with my hand when I spoke and bowing my head forward when walking past people, so my hair shrouded my face and hid the profile of my bulging lips.

When I was going to job interviews at 15 I trained myself to sit on my hands so that the potential employer wouldn't think there was something wrong with me as I spoke through my fingers.

I was also a terrible nail biter. My fingertips were bloody, chewed-off stumps. My mother painted my nails with foul-tasting 'Stop Bite', but it didn't work. To her credit she spared the money and took me to get artificial nails when they were first invented. But it didn't stop me from putting my fingers in my mouth and picking at the skin around my thumbs.

Everyone has stories about the challenges of growing up. Mine are what they are, and in writing about them, here, it mostly illustrates, for me, how far I've come in unraveling and releasing the mess of my childhood.

Growing up, writing was something I loved to do. I wrote in diaries – I still have all of them from when I was seven years old.

This is the first poem I wrote:

'My flowers run wild,
Every once in a while
Now is the while
So sit back and enjoy
While you can
As the gems of heaven sparkle
Bringing a rare and beautiful light
To the darkest corners of my garden.
As the souls of angels flutter down
Bringing a mystical whiteness
To the dark exotic night.'

I loved Enid Blyton's books. My dearest wish at Christmas was to receive the next instalment of *The Magic Faraway Tree* from Santa. I can remember feeling so incredibly thrilled unwrapping the book, and immediately I raced away to a quiet chair to read. I experienced unspeakable joy in the adventures of the cloud world at the top of the Faraway Tree. I'm sure Enid influenced my confidence that the natural world was indeed a completely magickal and spellbinding place, where I would spend most of my time if I could.

I remember feeling happy when a short story I wrote when I was 10 was selected for the school year book. I can remember it pretty much verbatim, 40 years later:

Isobel awoke to the boom of Admiral Jackson's cannon. She rushed to her bedroom window, pulling aside the thick drape … and saw a world carpeted in white. 'Snow!' she cried.

Still in her pajamas she ran to the front door, hauling on black rubber boots and a heavy ruby-red woolen coat. She opened the door, stepping down the steps and out onto a carpet of white ice.

Isobel walked along a corridor of trees, the sound of her crunching steps lulling her into a dreamy state. Snowflakes fluttered down from the sky, dusting her cheeks …

Queen Isobel is sitting in her throne. Around her, members of her court are having hushed conversations. She is dressed in a beautiful red gown lined with ermine fur. A small goblin approaches her, holding a tray with a glass of red wine. As he lifts his foot to step up to her throne he trips and the wine falls into Queen Isobel's lap.

Isobel awoke with a start, she had fallen asleep under a tree and a pile of snow had slid off a branch and into her lap.

It must be getting late! she thought, and quickly jumped up and ran home.

Home was somewhere my heroine ran to, but, growing up, 'home' didn't feel safe to me. A lot of places didn't. From a very young age, I was sexually abused by my grandfather. One of my earliest memories is being told to go and sit with him in the TV room at my grandparents' house while my mum and grandmother washed up after dinner. Grandpa would have *The Price is Right* turned up really loud on the TV and he would put his hand on my leg and then his fingers would creep up under my dress and into my underpants. He would breathe heavily and never take his eyes off the TV screen. I was very young; my first memory of this happening, my legs didn't even reach over the edge of the chair. This happened every time we went there and continued through the years when my legs could reach the floor. I never told anyone. I grew up thinking I was a yukky girl. My childhood logic was that 'yukky things happen to yukky girls'. I thought in some way I deserved it. Why else would it keep happening? It didn't occur to me to disobey my mother and not sit in there. In my youngest years I did what I was told. In my teens, at family gatherings, my grandfather would grab my breasts and stick his tongue in my ear. It was so disgusting.

Years later, my grandfather conveniently died of Alzheimer's and was never held accountable for what he did to me. I remember seeing him at a church event as his illness progressed. He stared blankly at me like he didn't know me. He said in a soft voice, 'How are you, love?'

I had terribly low self-esteem in my teens and if I wasn't naturally feeling it, I made sure I created reasons for it – choosing lousy dropkicks for boyfriends, hanging out with rebellious, mean kids, who I ran around after, seeking their approval while they rejected me. This was a pattern I had grown accustomed to. I wanted my parents to love me, but nothing I did was good enough or right enough. I loved trying new things and I would jump from idea to idea, project to project and, eventually, job to job! My father loved saying I was a 'jack of all trades, master of none'. So I sought more rejection. It's just what I learned to do.

I also purposely did badly in school so I wouldn't get picked on, and in an attempt to be liked I did dumb stunts like climbing from one classroom window into another classroom window – on the second floor – and taking a handful of allergy medication because some classmates said it was drugs and it would make me 'out of it' and cool. All it did was make me nod off in class, and the kids who had told me to take the medication pretended they didn't know me. I was taken to the head mistress's office and made to stand in a corner all day, nodding off, until my mother came to collect me. I was expelled.

I have a report card left over from that time which says: 'Fiona is a gifted but troubled child.'

As my father also liked to say often: 'You should have been put in a bucket.' He wasn't happy that they got me in the adoption lottery.

I realise this is a terribly dark way to start a book. Sitting here contemplating my childhood I feel, alternatively, like crying and erasing everything I've just written. Although not formally diagnosed, I've struggled with depression most of my life. Was I born with it? Or was it created and implanted into my behavioural patterns by the events and experiences I had throughout my childhood?

The good thing about having mostly bad and uncomfortable family memories is that it highlights the wonderful times I spent alone in my childhood.

To my mother's credit, she would make us kids go out and play in the bush when we got home from school. And it was in the (then) densely forested southern Sydney suburban bush that I had my first tangible, magickal experiences. I loved being in the bush – I trusted it and felt safe in nature. We were brought up to be careful of snakes and spiders, but I was never fearful – I only felt happy and free. I followed the trails and paths into the bush;

I knew where the waterfall was and where the rockpool with its lush moss edges lay. I made fairy gardens and left offerings for the frilled-neck lizards with their blue tongues whipping in and out (they were my favourite animals at the time). I climbed high up into trees and lay in their branches, smelling the aromatic eucalyptus leaves. It's still one of my very favourite smells. I collected pebbles and chunks of quartz crystal and kept them in secret spots in the crevices of tree branches and under loose bark.

One day I climbed up the steep face of a cliff over the river and found a small cave decorated with indigenous drawings. For a table I used an old plastic rubbish can that had been washed up on the riverbank, a piece of sandstone as a seat, and a broken bottle as a vase. I picked native flowers for my vase and filled it every week with water from the river. I was sure that, one day, I would live in the cave full time – safe. I was only 10 at the time. Because you needed to haul yourself five feet up the face of this rock on roots and vines, to get in, I was convinced no one would find me. My cave looked out over the Georges River, where I would sometimes go and chip oysters off the rocks along the river's edge. To this day I love eating raw oysters. I really, really loved the bush. I was being brought up in a strict Catholic school and attended church every Sunday, but in my heart I was a little Pagan.

My mother took great pride in her skills as a homemaker and I learned a lot from her how to run an orderly home. She was also so skilled at knitting and crocheting. Even though I have so many unhappy memories as a child, I remember loving the time Mum taught me to crochet and knit. She is such a passionate gardener too. To this day I have loved taking walks with Mum, looking at her garden and her telling me about what she is planting and growing. She really is the consummate homemaker. It's just that I was not the consummate daughter that she wanted.

But, nonetheless, she instilled in me good housekeeping skills and I leveraged this to my advantage when I made a deal with my parents from the age of 14 that I would not have to go to Mass if I cleaned the house. I loved my two hours alone at home on a Sunday morning, cleaning. I would play my Abba record and clean and clean. I took great pride in how lovely the house looked when my parents returned home. I still enjoy cleaning my living space, now, and keeping things spotless and organised.

As much as I poured my energy into having a beautiful, clean family home, it did not feel safe to me. My dreams were always nightmares. In a recurring dream a volcano would grow in our backyard. It would explode and hot lava would run over the lawn. I would run and run, as hard as I could, but I could not get off the lawn and away. I would wake up just as the lava engulfed me.

I also had a recurring dream about flying in a room full of boxes, with a man in a cape and top hat chasing me. I was terrified during the chase, but I loved the feeling of flying. Maybe this dream planted the seed for my eventual career as a commercial pilot. I didn't flap my arms like wings; I flew as if I were an aeroplane.

In my adult life I have been asked if I'm an adrenaline junkie. I don't think I am, but when I was young I loved jumping off things and pretending I was the Bionic Woman. On the backyard swing set I would rock myself higher and higher and jump at the very peak of the arc, enjoying the slow pull of gravity as I came off the 'hill of air' and plummeted to earth. Just like skydiving out of a hot-air balloon (I would discover years later).

Not all the adult relationships in my childhood were dysfunctional: I looked up to Sister Geraldine, a nun who was tough and cool and who bossed the boys back into line at my co-ed primary school; Mrs Hestalow, my Level 2 maths teacher told me I was really smart, and she was so proud of me when I did well in class that I couldn't bring myself to purposely fail the first term. As a result I was put in the Level 1 maths class, which I immediately failed so I could go back to Mrs Hestalow. Mrs Kahane was a really nice science teacher who made weathering and erosion so interesting that I forgot to purposely fail her class too. I really liked her knee-high leather boots, A-line skirts and pageboy haircut. I was such a big dag back then. I loved ABBA but I loved AC/DC too (the rock chick was peeking out, but she wouldn't fully emerge for few years).

There was one other guest teacher I remember having a good adult connection with. She taught an elective class – cosmetology – and she mentioned a new product that combined a shampoo and a conditioner. I remember putting my hand up and saying that I didn't think it could work because the shampoo would just wash out the conditioner, and she asked me if I did well in science because that was a smart thing to say. I remember the girls in the classroom mocking me afterwards, but I was secretly thrilled that this lady thought I was smart and didn't put me down for it.

I also remember my very first yoga class. It was a Friday afternoon elective. I was allocated this class because my preferred electives were full. I got lucky. To this day I can still feel the extraordinary sensation of the guided meditation. The teacher's voice prompted us to visualise colours with different temperatures flowing over our bodies. My unfettered child mind went off into a trippy hyperspace with my first meditation. The colours were so lush I could taste them in the back of my throat. I felt as if I were floating in a kaleidoscopic ocean. I was boiling-hot red, icy green, warm blue. I completely loved that yoga experience. It planted a seed deep inside me that I would cultivate later in life.

Despite not enjoying being the centre of attention and not having many friends, there is one pivotal memory from a school disco that I was allowed to attend. It was my first school social event and Olivia Newton John and John Travolta were the style king and queen from the movie *Grease*. Mum dressed me in a blue terry-toweling strapless jumpsuit. I carried a shiny red vinyl purse and wore red high-heeled wedgie shoes. I had Farrah Fawcett curls down the front of my long blonde hair. I loved my outfit but I was so nervous when I arrived at the public hall. All the boys were on one side of the room and all the girls on the other. I didn't know what to do, so I just stood there. And then the DJ announced a dance competition. The song was 'Rock Lobster' by the B-52's. I LOVED this song. My love of the song overcame my nerves and I went to the centre of the room and danced like a mad girl, shaking my head almost off my shoulders. And then as the singer called 'Down, down, down', I lay face-down on the floor … before getting back up and flinging my body all over the place again.

I won the competition.

There was another school dance I was allowed to attend a year later. This time it was at St Patrick's College, which was a boys school directly opposite Mary Immaculate College – the new high school I was attending. The most momentous thing about this dance was that it was the first time I got drunk. I had been allowed to latch myself onto a gang of tough girls and we were down at the basketball courts, smoking. I couldn't draw back without choking and was teased mercilessly about it. So, to make up for my lack of smoking skills they said I needed to scull a goonie bag of wine. Someone held it up and opened the geyser into my mouth. I dutifully guzzled it down. I must have drunk a litre of it.

The next thing I remember I was floating down to the school gymnasium. It was the most marvelous feeling. My feet didn't touch the earth. I felt confident and like I could do anything in the world. As the night went on the buzz remained and my last coherent memory is sitting on an older boy's lap, tongue-kissing him with my hand clumsily grasping between his legs. I was thirteen.

While I wasn't busted for that, I was busted for being drunk. My parents were called to drive me home. The next day I was the laughing-stock of the school and branded a slut, or 'frigid moll' to be exact. At the time this seemed like a contradiction, but I accepted the shameful branding and was more unhappy than ever.

I found solace in the Padstow Library. Mum would drop me off there while she went to shop, and I would head straight to the adult section. I would borrow armloads of books: *National Geographic* tomes on ancient cultures, the biography of Jayne Mansfield, and *Andra* – a novel about a girl who lived in the future and gave her life to save the world (it was my favourite book and I borrowed it multiple times. I saved up my pocket money to eventually buy it, and still have the original copy).

It was a biography of Jayne Mansfield that introduced me to Satanism. I read that she followed Anton LaVey and his Satanic Church and it all sounded so exotic and interesting and opposite to the world I was being brought up in. I wanted to look deeper into it. I don't remember how, but I got hold of a copy of *The Satanic Bible* (maybe I borrowed it from the library, but it seems unlikely because my mum checked everything I borrowed).

I tried saying the Lord's Prayer backwards and conjuring up demons by candlelight, who would fly me away on their spiky wings ...

But nothing happened and the more I read about it, the more it seemed like the Catholic Church I was being forced to attend. Torture and weirdness, control and the sex stuff, was all creepy to my young mind. So I decided Satanism wasn't for me. I wasn't sure what was.

The beautiful confirmation dress my mother sewed – it did not convince me that being Catholic was for me.

I would retreat to the bush – the one place of peace – although it wasn't so peaceful anymore: some teenage boys had become aware of me. On my walk home after being dropped off by the school bus, one guy would follow me in his white panel van. Slowly creeping behind me. I became so paranoid that I would jump into the bush and find my way home by cutting through the thick scrub, less worried about poisonous snakes than I was about this guy finding me and dragging me into his van.

One day I was wandering in the bush, heading back home from my cave by the river, when I heard a snicker. I realised two boys were watching me from a few bushes away. I ran all the way home.

They didn't follow me, but the next day I went down to my cave and it was ruined. My little table display was smashed, the upside-down bin was floating on the shore, having been tossed out, and there was horrible graffiti of penises and swear words scraped into the rock with powdery shale.

My sanctuary in the bush was gone. But soon I would be, too. I would find my solace in other places. It's something I was driven to search for as I travelled out into the world.

Somewhere in the middle of all this awkward boy stuff I met an older boy. He was the DJ at the local rollerskating rink. He looked like Jimmy Barnes from Cold Chisel (in those days, that meant 'hot').

He would flash a toothy smile at me and, microphone in hand, dedicate Skyhooks' 'I See Red' to the 'blonde in the KISS Army t-shirt and the red shorts' and I would skate around the rink as fast as I could, hoping that no one noticed the bulge in my shorts from my maxi pad (my mum would not let me use tampons).

One day he drove me away from the roller rink to the Sutherland Shire National Park and had sex with me. He put tea-towels up in the windows of his yellow Torana GTR XU1, pulled down my pants and stuck the neck of a Coke bottle inside me. He said it was sexy. I didn't know what to do. I wanted to appear cool, but it felt awful. He got the bottle in about an inch and then with his fingers he pushed at the lips between my legs and said, 'If you just had these cut off you'd be perfect.' Then he put his penis inside me.

He couldn't get it all the way in because I was a virgin.

After that he took me to Kentucky Fried Chicken. I remember really enjoying the chicken.

○

As I write this at the age of 50, I can see that everything I have done in recent years has been an attempt to right the wrongs of my childhood. Including never ever eating KFC again.

But as I sit here in a 400-year-old restored home owned by my friends, in Old San Juan, a Spanish colonised island in the Caribbean, and bang away at this laptop, I consider whether my life is defined by sadness or by joy.

For decades I was convinced that you had to pay for happiness with sadness. One week of happiness cost three weeks of sadness.

I was absolutely convinced that this was necessary and the way of the world. I was so convinced of it that I made it happen.

Incredibly, I can see now that I no longer think this way. I have learned to discipline my mind and cut away a lot of that negative reinforcement. It took years, no, *decades*, to train it away.

The same challenging life stuff happens, but I react to it differently. As children, we become 'adult'erated. Altered from a state of joy and excited anticipation for the adventure in life, to becoming a creature that expects the worst, or, at the very least, expects a high price to be paid for a little joy. And, adding to that, we become adulterated to think that everything can be bought with money. But it's not the case. I've learned that, too. And at this point in my life I can say I am very wealthy in heart and life experiences … whilst being cash poor!

chapter two

A GIFTED BUT TROUBLED CHILD

'Alone, always alone
Turned in upon myself
I open up to a great expanse
Released of all my mortal traps
I fly
Recognizing what is me
I face my own divinity
And in doing so I am free.'

For a brief time at the age of 14 or so, I was sent to a Marist Brothers school for troubled children. We were allowed to smoke if we had a letter of permission from our parents (I didn't have one but I snuck ciggies anyway. By this time I was doing the 'drawback'), and we went to school in six-week shifts: from 8 am to 2 pm for six weeks, then from 11 am to 5 pm for the next six weeks. It was supposed to get us used to shift work and getting a trade labour job when we left school.

One guy, Mark, had repeated so many times, he was 18 and could legally buy alcohol. I liked when he and I had the same school shift because he would take our orders and go and buy all the alcohol at the bottle-o, after school. Then I would get on the two-hour train ride home, which transferred at the rough inner-city station, Redfern. I would purposefully miss my connecting train so I could sit in the dark at the far end of the station, drinking from the hip flask, enjoying the warm sensation of the liquor going straight into my belly, as I listened to the Moody Blues' 'Knights in White Saturn' on my little yellow transistor radio and planned my eventual suicide.

Cultivating suicidal thoughts made me feel deep. The dark emotions were so intoxicating and I liked feeling intoxicated by anything – anything that could take me away from the reality of my life thus far.

I have so many memories of being shunned and ridiculed; I can still feel the sting of getting off the school bus and all the cool girls turning their backs on me. I remember the torture of the school bus, the jeering voices, the things that were thrown at me – books and oranges. I remember knowing I needed to leave home and get far, far away from all these people.

During that time in the school for troubled children, I also remember writing a piece about a waterfall, for my English requirement. I got a high mark. The teacher commented that I was a gifted writer. I also remember having a crush on two boys: one looked like Sid Vicious and liked sewing; one looked like Tom Cruise and liked motorbikes.

I didn't finish Year 10, didn't get my school certificate. Didn't do any final exams. I just got out.

The night I left home I can remember like yesterday. My car-loving, dropkick boyfriend, Richard, came and picked me up. My mother was saying, 'Don't you dare take anything we bought.' So I left with the clothes on my back and a toothbrush.

I had found a place to stay in the western suburb of Homebush. I would pay $50 a week to rent a bed in a room with three other girls and receive a hot meal at the end of the day. The house was split in half by a long hallway. Girls on one side, boys on the other. We were a motley, messy bunch. The husband and wife who ran the house also ran a brothel in Bondi and asked if I would come and work the front desk 'and maybe do some other stuff in the bedrooms.' I was working at Sydney City Smash Repairs at the time. I had got a job in a car repairs place because I was desperately seeking

Richard's approval. I was being trained to use an orbital sander, mix paint primer, and colour match. At lunchtime I would sit in the small, windowless lunchroom with the other men, surrounded by *Penthouse* centrefolds stuck on the wall, and we would eat our falafel rolls. The guys were polite enough, but the shared toilet was horrible. I tried to be cool and fit in. I wanted to be able to see Richard on the weekends and impress him with my knowledge of cars. But I was doomed with Richard. On those weekend visits, when he would get on top of me to have sex, I would just lie there. He would say, 'Can't you move or do something?' And I would say, 'What am I supposed to do?'

So I wouldn't have been much use working in a brothel.

I had to get out of that horrible Homebush house – the night one of its inhabitants went mad with an axe and smashed up his VW in the driveway was enough – and so I went and lived at my grandparents'. It was the only option I had in order to move quickly. I was not welcome at the house I grew up in. I was older, now, I reasoned, and I could avoid my grandfather's groping. And my grandmother was so lovely and would make her secret-recipe fruit-mince pies for me sometimes. Their house was on a train line and I was able to get to work in the city easily enough.

One day as I was heading home from work wearing my paint-splattered overalls, a woman sat down next to me.

I remember sneaking a glance at her and thinking she had the most beautiful profile I had ever seen. She had a dark red bob. She turned to me, her luminous green eyes penetrating mine, and said, 'Have you ever thought of being a model?'

I remember putting my head down and laughing and saying I was too ugly. But the lady, Cheryl, insisted I wasn't and that she would like to help me become a model. I gave her my grandparents' phone number and got off the train, heart pounding and head spinning.

Modeling seemed so glamorous and fabulous; I read *Dolly* magazine and *Sixteen* – I used to borrow them from the Bexley North Library. The thought of being in them was extraordinary to me.

Cheryl arranged for me to have my hair cut at a fancy hair salon in the Strand Arcade. I remember walking in and feeling so inadequate. Eddie washed and conditioned my hair with expensive shampoo and conditioner. My mother had only let me use Sunlight soap on my hair and I always had a tangled and matted ball of hair at the back of my head. But now the comb glided through my fine hair like silk. Eddie also gave me my first head massage, before cutting my hair into bangs. I remember everyone oohing and aahing about how fabulous I looked. My previous experience of haircuts was the Illawong local hairdresser, 'Hack Em Up Harvey' as she used to be called, who cut your hair at her home.

Now I sort of, maybe, looked a little bit like a model. My hair was so blonde and shiny.

Cheryl was a very successful model – she was starring in a big contact-lens campaign (contact lenses were very new at the time). She paid for me to have some photos taken for my 'portfolio'. I felt so dorky and uncomfortable in front of the camera. The photos were okay, but not great. She told me I should sign up to a modeling and deportment course.

The two most reputable deportment schools were Madame Korner College and the June Dally-Watkins School. June Dally-

Watkins was one train stop closer to me, so I signed up there for a two-week course.

In all these years I have never Googled June Dally-Watkins, but I just did as I'm writing this! She is still the Queen of Deportment. Here is an advertisement for one of the classes from her site, posted in 2017, which is pretty much the same as it was back in the 80s:

www.junedallywatkins.com.au
Make-over Programme
Let us unveil your natural beauty with expert advice!
We will revitalise your:
- *Deportment – How to sit and stand correctly.*
- *Make fashion work for you. Discover styles for your body shape. Feel a new lease of life with your personal colour analysis.*
- *Skin Analysis, skin care and product advice.*
- *Be shown the tips and tricks of make-up application (day-night).*
- *Find out which hairstyle will best suit you (optional visit to hairdresser at a time to suit you, $60).*

After being trained to walk and put on make-up by Miss Dally-Watkins herself, Cheryl got me representation at her agency and I was sent on a couple of castings.

I remember one was for a Clearasil commercial. At the audition I found myself getting changed into a bikini in the toilets with Elle MacPherson, long before she became a supermodel. This was her first casting, too. She was so confident and I just felt like a dumb, ugly dork. She got the job, I didn't.

I remember feeling very intimidated by all the good-looking teens surrounding me. They seemed so comfortable with themselves. As each of us walked in the door, someone took a polaroid of us and we had to hang onto the picture and hand it in as we went into the actual casting. A very good-looking boy next to me looked at mine and then looked at my face and then back at the photo and said, 'You look okay from certain angles. I guess you're a bit photogenic.' I wasn't sure what photogenic meant at the time but I felt stupid and embarrassed regardless. 'Good but not good enough,' was what I heard.

Modeling turned into more of an experience in manipulation. Cheryl and Eddie were on again/off again boyfriend and girlfriend; she ended up encouraging me to have sex with him. I was useless and inexperienced. Desperately seeking approval, though, I did what she suggested.

This taste of the modeling world, however, had me want to get out of car repairs and I applied for a job as a researcher on a TV soap called *The Young Doctors*. I showed up at the office for the meeting, my examples of writing and reports from school, attesting to my English skills, in hand. I was sent into a room where a woman handed me a bikini. She told me to put it on. I said, 'What does this have to do with researching?' She said, 'Oh I thought you were here for the audition for a role!' I said, 'No – the researcher.' She said, 'Well, let's just take a few photos of you and get something on camera anyway.'

So I did that.

And then I had my job interview for the script researcher position. I got the job. I was only sixteen years old so I had to get a letter of permission from my parents.

But Mum and Dad were so furious that I had been photographed in a bikini that they did not give me permission to accept the job. They said it was too fancy and not a real job. It was such a shame. My life could have taken a turn for the better, in a job doing something that used my brain in the way it should have been used. Deep down I loved reading and learning and writing. But I was forbidden to accept the job. My father said I should look for a proper job, like be a 'sexy-tary' (as in secretary). It was the 80s and sexism was rife and expected. He also said I should be a flight attendant. Funnily enough, four decades later I became a professional pilot.

Back at 'home' I tried to avoid my grandfather and his groping. My grandmother was such a sweet lady and I enjoyed being around her. But ultimately, she told me I needed to leave because other members of the family were saying I shouldn't be getting special treatment and be allowed to stay at Grandma and Grandpa's. I remember one aunty coming to me at a family gathering and saying, 'Your mother will never love you as much as I love my children. You're not really hers. You're not really anyone's, are you?' At the time, I liked listening to The Clash. The song 'Should I Stay or Should I Go' echoed through my head a lot as she thrust her face into mine.

I left. And her daughter moved into Grandma and Grandpa's straight away.

I found a place to rent in Kings Cross – a bedsit in Billyard Ave; I didn't have a view of the water but I was in the eastern suburbs and renting a single room with a hotplate and a small fridge and shared bathroom for $40 a week. I had moved on from westie dropkick Richard – I was never going to earn his love.

This fact sunk in one day in his garage in Blacktown: After being egged on by his friends saying that Richard would think it was cool, I pulled a giant bucket cone of pot and skulled a litre of milk straight after. I felt so sick and it didn't distract Richard from making out with another girl right in front of me.

I got a job working as a house model at Leon Cutler. I would answer phones and model the size-10 wardrobe if buyers came in to see the latest collection. But that didn't last long. I felt too insecure to model and decided I wanted to travel, so I got a job at a travel agency, as a receptionist. I had thought that maybe I could see the world if I worked there. But my job didn't last long: I went to work one day in thongs because someone had stolen all my shoes.

I had been letting a gay prostitute friend named Gary use my apartment as a place to see his clients (one of which stole my shoes) whilst I drank downstairs at the Rex Hotel. I was sixteen, but no one had to show ID in those days. I was drinking and popping pills and making out with girls from the chest up because being gay was cool. My best friends were drag queens, trannies and gay street kids.

I started to descend into street life, too. My seventeenth year is a bit of a blur. I was taking drugs – just pills and pot – and getting fired and then finding a new job pretty much every month. In some ways this lifestyle was wild, free and fun, but it was not sustainable. I lost my apartment and ended up sleeping in the Kings Cross toilets for a month.

I remember a really smelly punk guy with spiked black hair licking my face one night, in an attempt at foreplay. I realised I couldn't bear living on the streets anymore, hanging around the

Four Corners Chicken Shop hoping some guy would take pity on me and buy me half a roast chicken for dinner. I can't remember how I made the leap to getting a job and renting an apartment again, but I did.

I ended up in Surry Hills, renting a room in a shared apartment, and I started going to see grungy bands. The lead singer of one of my favourite bands was a dark-haired, dark-eyed English girl. She was the first person to put a needle in my arm. I wasn't sure if I liked the feeling heroin gave me, but I liked being her friend, even though our friendship was mainly built on the fact that I had a job and an income and could buy heroin for her as well as for myself.

Her band played one night at the Strawberry Hills Hotel, which was in my neighbourhood. I remember she and I fishing around in her dirty duffel bag for a pick (street talk for needle). We mixed up the heroin on the underside of a beer can, sitting on the back of the toilet. She stuck the needle in her arm and then in mine. It was so blunt she had to stab it into me roughly ten times before it struck a vein. But I got a hit. Then she went and performed. Her band was supporting The Gun Club, which was my very favourite band at the time, and I was in love with their lead singer, Jeffrey Lee Pierce. She scored him heroin after the show. He died of an overdose some years later. Around this time I also started shooting up speed, which I liked more than heroin, but I was doing both.

There is a blurry year when I worked in the royalties department at Warner Chappell Music in Woolloomooloo. I would go home at lunchtime and hit up speed – I never put the needle in my arm myself, though. I couldn't bring myself to. I always asked someone else to do it. By this time I was sharing a house on Woomerah Ave, in Darlinghurst, with members of my heroin friend's band, and dating her old boyfriend. The drummer was always home and he would stick me with a needle. I would go back to work, my teeth grinding and heart racing, and plough through those giant sheets of paper, checking off Elton John's royalty payments at lightning speed – my bosses were amazed with the volume I could churn out.

I was living on the edge, but there was one fabulous reassuring and safe thing about this time in my life. I met Lydia. She was working as a temp for Warner Chappell and we struck up a friendship. Lydia wanted to be a nurse. She eventually did become one and, now, thirty-three years later, we are still friends and she is a Registered Specialist Nurse in cancer nursing. I love Lydia. And after all these years she looks exactly the same! She was a stabilising presence in my life. On the weekends she and I would dress up in our best grunge punk threads and take photos of each other around the city – starring in our own campaign of fabulousness. It was fun. Lydia also went on to be a celebrated photographer in addition to her work helping her patients.

At some point during this year, my parents kind of came to the rescue. I was high one night and I called Mum from a Town Hall Station payphone. I had left my job at Warner Chappell (or maybe I was fired, I don't remember). I had no money and was begging for food again. I developed agoraphobia after lining up for a pie at the Robertson Street Salvation Army kitchen. I took a bite of the pie and realised there was mold all over it. Or maybe I was hallucinating. Whatever it was, all of a sudden I couldn't bear the weight of the sky. I curled into a ball, huddled against a curb on the street corner. When I eventually felt I could move, I crawled along the street, hugging the curb. Everything seemed so insanely large and I was so small. I thought I was dead, but I was too terrified to be dead. For all my risk-taking I was actually really scared of dying. And I was really fucked up. Something inside of me was giving me a wake-up call. As I crawled along the street like a mad woman, there was a voice screaming in my head:

'FIONA THIS ISN'T YOU! THIS IS NOT YOUR LIFE! STOP THIS!'

Somehow I ended up at the train station. And I called my mum. We arranged to meet at Central Station the next day. I wore a short-sleeved t-shirt so she could see the tracks on my arms. We drank coffee at the restaurant. And I returned home with her.

I had developed drug-induced psychosis. I was quite insane. I was freezing cold all the time and had a constant urge to urinate. I had terrible panic attacks, which would cause me to collapse. My heart would pound so hard in my chest that I asked my mother to lie down on top of me so that her weight would prevent my heart breaking out of my chest. I would be shaking, sweating, my heart pounding, and begging her to talk to me about anything that could take my mind off the insane fear that life itself was consuming me. She would talk to me about the sewing classes she was planning to take me to.

Life became black and white, literally. I lost my ability to see colours. I couldn't smell. Everything looked two-dimensional. Even people looked flat, like cartoons. Anytime I spoke to someone I would carefully look behind them to see if they had depth and shape, otherwise they looked like flat drawings. I wasn't sure if the people I was talking to were really there.

I managed to get a temp job with a government department – I think it was, ironically, the Department of Health. There wasn't much for me to do.

Because I was freezing all the time, I wore a big thick green coat that I had bought in an op shop for three dollars. I also wore skirts because I was always running to the bathroom. I had a big Honeywell computer to work on, and loaded onto it was *Adventure*, the original fantasy role-playing computer game. I spent the months working there typing the occasional letter for my boss and unraveling the hidden secrets of *Adventure*, ending up in the dragon's lair with all the jewels having defeated the evil goblins … or something like that. Actually, I never finished it. I was still very conscious that I was good but not good enough and I could never be a true success at anything. I was all 'smoke and mirrors', an almost-but-not-quite girl. I couldn't even become a full-blown heroin addict. I never got all the way with *Adventure* – but two guys in the office next to me did. They even mapped out the crazy maze. I remember looking at the printout of it and thinking, there's no way I could ever work that out – I never stick at anything long enough.

I would get home from work at night and have another panic attack – convinced I was dying – and my mother would take me to a local doctor who would see me at night. I told the doctor I was too scared to take painkillers for the crippling headaches I was suffering because I was scared someone would have made a mistake at the factory and I would take a poison pill, not a headache pill. I was lucky this doctor understood me. She gave me a book: *Relief Without Drugs* by Ainslie Meares. I read it and his wisdom on how to deal with anxiety, terror and panic, without drugs, resonated. As I took the steps suggested in the book, I slowly started to get better. My sense of smell returned, colours reappeared and people were less terrifying.

I discovered a store called The Tree of Life, on George St near where I worked. I spent my lunchtimes there, smelling the incense, reading the esoteric books on the shelves, holding crystals in my hands. It wasn't the bush setting of my childhood, but it had the same feeling – a sense of magic; a sense of being a safe haven.

At home, my father called me Fat Head (after my initials, F.H.), and yet, mysteriously, he also did something really wonderful for me: he sent me to a weekend writers workshop at Bathurst University. I loved waking up in the morning and walking under the eucalyptus trees before heading into the classroom. I stayed in a dormitory there for three nights, with other wannabe writers. Our task was to complete a 1500-word story that would be read to the class at the end of the weekend.

I wrote about my life on the street. I remember, after reading it, there was silence in the room. I think I shocked people. I could function conveniently in society, and I think the other participants saw me as a nice, polite girl who could not have lived that life. The teacher said I should continue writing.

Even though my father has, more often than not, expressed his displeasure at my existence, I am extremely grateful for this moment where our energies combined harmoniously and he helped me know that I could write things that other people would want to read.

My temp job at the Department of Health came to an end and I moved out of home again. There was too much tension for everyone. The paranoia and panic attacks continued intermittently for a few years, but I could sense the warning signals when my brain would start to go to 'that place' and I would start to get tunnel vision. I would take a deep breath and, most of the time, I would be able to stop the attack coming on.

In the blur of my years from 18 to 21, I worked in a clothing store called Dotti, a health-food store in Martin Place, a sandwich shop in Strand Arcade and a bar in Circular Quay, where our uniform was a white t-shirt with no bra. I also moved to Adelaide for a brief period, chasing my old junkie boyfriend Jim (although I didn't do heroin again). I also met a fabulous girl named Wendy, and despite having meagre skills as a guitarist, taught her to play bass and we formed a grunge garage punk band with our boyfriends, called Sister Sludge. I had decided I didn't want to follow bands anymore – I wanted to be in one. I had taught myself to play guitar using the chord chart of 'Space Oddity' by David Bowie, and had painstakingly picked out the chords on a cheap guitar for months until I felt confident enough to write my own song.

Sister Sludge had developed a bit of a following in Adelaide – we were loud, obnoxious and enthusiastic. We played with bands like Lubricated Goat, Salamander Jim and The Johnnies. Wendy and I would chug a bottle of Tia Maria off the side of the stage to get confidence to go on (yuk!) and, in order to lose weight, we ate only vegemite, cheese and tomato on toast. We drank coffee, smoked Winnie Reds and ate one toasted sandwich in the evening for dinner. We were always slightly skinny, slightly nauseous and slightly fabulous in those Adelaide daze, as we ploughed through op shops with teased beehive hair and thick black eyeliner. We found 60s and 70s threads like fake-fur-trimmed and fringed vests, ancient lace corsets, paisley tights, and knee-high lace-up boots, and we stomped around in our grungy glam wardrobe at work during the day and while rocking out on stage at night.

But Adelaide got too small for us and Wendy and I decided to move back up to Sydney together, into a house on Walker St in Redfern. Wendy found work as a graphic artist and got very busy being very good at her job. Sister Sludge ended. I started another band – an all-girl punk band called The Mothers. The feminist in me was resisting patriarchal society by calling us The Mothers, as in child bearers, and also The Mothers as in motherfuckers. Wendy became our photographer and cover artist for the music we would eventually release.

We 'Mothers', Nat, Jo and I, would jam and write songs around the kitchen table in our little house at Redfern – Nat and I on guitar and Jo banging on the table as drums. It was fun. My old girlfriend from Illawong, Linda, moved in with Wendy and me. She was one of the happy memories from my time growing up in the suburbs. I remember we used to hang out at her house on a Saturday and come up with dance routines to songs from the album *Saturday Night Fever* (which had been hot at the time). Her parents allowed her to have multiple vinyl records – she had an awesome music collection – and her dad was a drummer. I used to love the freedom of expression encouraged at Linda's home. She and I had got up to some trouble together in the Shire and our parents eventually forbade us to be friends. So, it was

Wendy and I before going onstage in our band, Sister Sludge.

great to hang out, now, as young adults. She was a hairdresser. We would all take acid some nights ('Blue Pyramid' anyone?) and I remember once riding my push bike at 4 am to work at a fancy sandwich shop in the Strand Arcade, still tripping off my head. When it came time to put the roast beef on the slicer I thought I was cutting up a human leg. That's when I decided to become vegetarian. I remained vegetarian, as I became more educated about the evils of the food industry and also to buck the establishment, but, at the start it was just because I was tripping.

There were no more needles for me in the Walker St days, but there were packets of speed every Friday night. It was just what we did: score, do some lines, get dressed-up and head on down to the Sydney Trade Union Club. The speed made me feel confident, like I could talk to anyone. I was no longer the tongue-tied shy girl. I had a line and I'd waffle on. Like everyone else, pretty much.

There were so many great bands playing back then, and I was usually crushing on someone in one of them. I remember Brett, from The Died Pretty, breaking my heart; he slept with me and then went back to his girlfriend – multiple times. He was really into Andy Warhol and the Velvet Underground. I tried to impress him by covering the ceiling of my bedroom with alfoil, but he never came over to see it. No matter what I did I wasn't good enough to be loved and approved by the person I hoped would accept me. I realise now that I was manifesting the rejection of the first man who broke my heart – my father.

Stu from Lubricated Goat came over and got into my bed, but I kicked him out because his feet stank. He told me a couple of years later that I hurt his feelings when I did that. I guess I was a bit of a heartbreaker after all.

Over the next year, I set simple goals. The Mothers recorded a 7-inch single on the Waterfront Records label. The song was called 'Drives Me Wild' and I wrote it about my boyfriend Blackie who was the guitarist for the Hard-Ons.

When I see you, standing there, baggy jeans and curly hair
When I look into your blue, blue eyes – it drives me wild, drives
   me wild, yeah!

For a while we were in love and when the Redfern house ended, I moved in with Blackie, back to where I started, in the yobbo western suburb of Auburn. Blackie was a sweet guy and the Hard-Ons were really popular. He was also vegetarian and really into running. I started running, too, and used to love getting up early and putting on my Walkman, with Sepultura, early Metallica, and Suicidal Tendencies, and running fast and hard around the streets of Auburn and Strathfield.

To get Blackie to like me I used to sneak out on my lunch

My best friend, Wendy Hannam's wonderful cover art.

break and go to the Petersham Hotel, where he used to hang out a lot, and practise playing the pin-ball machine there over and over again until I could easily pop it.

Then, on a Friday night when I saw him, I would be the cool girl who could 'pop the pinny'. It didn't matter that I was the lead singer in The Mothers and that we had our own little following. I would practise popping that pinny until I got Blackie. And I did.

The Mothers was still up and running after the success of our 7-inch single, and playing shows up and down the east coast, driving the twelve hours between Sydney and Melbourne on multiple weekends in a crappy van.

We recorded a 12-inch single called '12-incher', with a new line-up – a cool girl named Cris on bass, and two boys, Rick and Luke, on drums and guitar. We shot the cover at the urinal in St James Station with all of us lined up and Cris and I 'taking a piss' with the boys.

It was a funny, dorky cover. It was my idea. I was wearing a Stevie Nicks 'Belladonna' tour t-shirt. Cris was a little skinhead with big cat's eyes and a number 1 buzz cut. She was edgy and cool. I was stuck between a surf punk and Agnetha from Abba – still a big dag playing cool and desperately seeking approval and acceptance.

It was the mid 80s and I was hungrily exploring metaphysical things popularised by the New Age movement. As much as I was trying to be an edgy, rough, rocker punk, I was also loving meditation and Louise Hay books. I had my first tangible out-of-body experience in the apartment in Auburn, with Blackie. I was meditating using a guided recording playing on a little cassette deck. Suddenly I felt myself shoot up into the air. I 'opened' my eyes and I could see my feet far below me. I closed my eyes again and I moved across the city over to Sydney Harbour and Manly Beach. I descended into the water and could feel its cool wetness flowing swiftly by me before I bumped my head on something. It was the hull of a boat. Suddenly I opened my physical eyes and I was back sitting at the base of my bed in Auburn. This was such a tangible experience that I caught the train into the city the next day and took the ferry across to Manly. I wanted to see if there was a boat moored offshore. There was. A tanker – lined up awaiting entry into Sydney Harbour. Maybe I really did hit my etheric head on the hull of that boat. I decided that I did. And I continued to explore New Age phenomena with relish.

Coming back from Manly that day I was standing at Manly Wharf, looking at people running in and running out of the turnstiles like harried ants. I had a feeling like I knew what I wanted to be. I wanted to have a shimmering blue aura and when people came into my physical proximity they would feel good. They would feel healed.

I thought this would be a good reason to live.

Just as my esoteric self was exploding, my love life imploded – Blackie and I hit a rough patch and he started seeing another girl, and I moved out.

I went in search of a more natural, earthy environment that would better reflect my spiritual self, and ended up near Manly Beach. I got a job managing the front desk at a gym in nearby North Sydney. I was reading more and more New Age and esoteric material and I was increasingly drawn to alternative ways of living. I studied naturopathy, saving up my wage to pay

6 am start every day opening the 1812 gym – a line of coke always helped after a late night of band practice.

for tuition at a private college called NatureCare. My inner Witch was trying to make herself heard and guided me towards being a healer. I loved going to college and studying herbal medicine, iridology and remedial massage, after work.

I used to get up at 5.30 am to catch the bus from Manly to North Sydney, open the gym and work until 2 pm, go to college until 7 pm and then band practice from 8 pm to midnight. Then I'd catch the bus back to Manly and sleep four hours and do it all again. I used to have an icy-cold shower to wake me up in the mornings and then get on the bus and listen to Pink Floyd on my Walkman, falling asleep until I reached my stop half an hour later.

The time working at the gym and studying naturopathy also coincided with a weird stretch of me getting into Ecstasy – it was new and very popular in the late 80s and everyone was rolling. That time is a bit of a blur except that everyone I knew seemed to be falling in love and getting engaged. But it was just the E.

The Mothers had a few more big shows and then ground to a halt. I was the only one blowing wind in the sails. The other band members decided they were out. I was disappointed but let it go. As it happened, I had caught someone's eye and my music career turned a big corner.

chapter three

WE ARE SURFERS OF THE MIND

'And the wise witch wove her dreams …
Spinning coiled ropes of silver that wound round the trees.
Starry eyed I'm spinning … slowly … a spiral dance.'

t was 1990 and I was sitting on the first floor of the Sydney Trade Union Club drinking a gin and tonic and wearing a top hat, Dead Kennedys t-shirt, a lace shawl and a floor-length skirt (looking Witch-like but I was still just scratching the surface) when the co-founder of what was to be Def FX approached me. He'd seen me perform in The (now-defunct) Mothers and asked if I wanted to collaborate on an idea he had – a hard-rock band that was backed by programmed dance beats rather than a drummer. It was intriguing and I agreed to be the lead singer of what became known as a cutting-edge and completely unique electronic rock band. We were part of a wave that launched a brand-new genre of music – commonly known now as 'Electronica' – first taking the Australian indie scene by storm and ultimately growing into a Top 40 commercial act.

We wrote two songs: 'Surfers of the Mind' and 'Sex Game Sucker' and entered them into the Yamaha/MTV music competition. Out of 400 entries we made it to the finals! We had barely become a band and we were going to be performing on national TV!

Alison, the host of MTV, came to film a pre-show interview with us in the garage of our guitarist Blake's home – we were being touted as a 'garage band' and MTV were taking it literally. I remember all of us sitting on a mattress on the floor, me looking quite smug next to the co-founder, who was extremely smug (once again I was people-pleasing and mirroring the attitudes of those around me in a desperate attempt for approval, and to belong). Marty (our bass player) and Blake were so stoned they couldn't stop giggling. When Alison asked how long we had been playing together I said, 'Not long. That's the secret; you don't have to "pay your dues", you just do it.' And I have been paying my dues for that statement ever since!

I made costumes for our performance, in the sink in the share laundry where I lived. I tie-dyed long-sleeved shirts for the boys and made a t-shirt and skirt from a cut-up t-shirt, for myself. I ironed sparkling transfers of zodiac signs and unicorns onto the tie-dyed fabric. I had cropped blonde hair, but for the performance I wore a long pink wig and a hand tie-dyed bandanna. I wore little black lace-up shoes and short socks ... The dag in me was still managing to make herself known.

TV legend Richard Wilkins, still sporting glorious, puffy 80s hair, was the host of the live event broadcast from the Coogee Bay Hotel.

We didn't win – a soft metal band did. But we got Best Newcomer Award and received a plaque presented to us by Australian music legend Michael Gudinski.

That led to getting a manager, being signed by EMI Records, and being a successful and professional charting band. Just like that.

For the next seven years I lived out of a suitcase, repeatedly touring Australia, the USA and Japan, playing not only in every dive bar, wild pub and packed RSL club with other Aussie bands such as Tumbleweed, You Am I, and Nitocris, but also every giant festival such as Big Day Out, and Livid. We also toured internationally with Nine Inch Nails, No Doubt, Soundgarden and The Smashing Pumpkins.

I learned to snuggle up in a Tarago, with two pillows, a doona, some potato chips and a beer. And off to sleep for the eight-hour drive I would go. Eventually we started flying everywhere. But there was something comforting about that Tarago van. I didn't have my driver's licence but sometimes the boys would be too out of it to drive, so I would. I was the one who didn't drink much or do drugs – incredibly I had a big 'about-face' while in the band. The shows were so grueling and I put it on myself to be so high energy, so full-on – screaming over the top of the crazy-loud backing tapes and guitars – that I didn't indulge in anything before the show, and often after, because I couldn't afford to be hungover with the rigorous six-shows-in-five-days touring schedule we often had.

The guys, on the other hand, were the rock stars, and partied hard all the way. I remember one time we played in Byron Bay and they (including our manager, who was just a boy) went to a rave on Whites Beach. They were still tripping hard when it came time to drive the rental van back down to Sydney in order to meet our return deadline. So I drove. We took an inland road, where there were likely to be fewer cops. I remember stopping for an ice-cream and to pee at Taree, four hours into the drive, and being proud of my 45-degree reverse parking. All the boys, meanwhile, were passed out. Our manager woke up about an hour out of Sydney and took over. The boys actually said 'Thanks

The national newspapers said, 'We don't know if Fiona Horne knew
she was making a powerful feminist statement when she removed
her top at Sydney's (1992) Big Day Out.' I did. Photo: Tony Mott

Fi' and 'Good job', as they fell out of the van when we reached our respective homes.

I should explain why I didn't have a licence: I left home very young and tended to live in the thick of things – everything was in walking distance. So I relied on buses, trains and occasionally taxis, for years. And I walked everywhere. When I wanted to get out of town I would catch the two-hour local Greyhound bus up to Palm Beach, or even further up the New South Wales coast to Pacific Palms, and stay in a caravan park on the beach.

When Def FX became really popular we were always being driven or given cab charges. This went on for a long time. I didn't get my driver's licence until I was 31 and had moved to Los Angeles. I was convinced I would never be able to confidently operate large vehicles (and now I fly planes! All that was ultimately required was a shift in attitude).

Back on the road …

The fun was often lost for me because I was the only girl on the road with a bunch of misogynistic boys. I remember chatting to Gwen Stefani about this, backstage at a gig with No Doubt in Tokyo (Blink 182 opened for us that night!). I was a bit awestruck because No Doubt's single 'Just A Girl' had become a huge worldwide hit. But she was very sweet and we took solace in each other's company, being the only two girls in the fifteen-man line-up. She asked me if I had a boy at home and I said, 'No. I am suffocated by men on the road as it is. I like to be alone when I can. How about you?' And she said she had just met a nice guy called Gavin. He turned out to be her future husband.

For nearly all of our seven years I didn't have a relationship with anyone except the other Def FX members. First the guitarist,

Blake, who unfortunately lost the plot on our first US tour because of the hectic schedule, a fragile state of mind, and our American tour manager, who pumped him full of laced pot. He went back to Australia and we lost our US record deal. Then, for a period, I was the co-founder's girlfriend. I guess it is inevitable if you are spending so much time together, on the road in our case, and you are in the reproductive phase of your life, your hormones churning, that you would date close to home.

The only other guy in all those years I had a significant connection with was Billy Corgan from The Smashing Pumpkins. There were a lot of rumours going around that we were boyfriend and girlfriend, but when I met him during a Big Day Out tour, he had just married and our bond was forged in friendship.

He took me out to dinner in Perth one night. I was a rock star but a major, insecure dork. His band was so huge – it was the time of *Siamese Dream* and 'Zero'. He still had curly hair. I wore a denim mini-skirt, black stockings, high-heeled wedgies and a red singlet top. Trying to look skinny and pretty. The boys in my band all snickered at me as I walked out of the hotel.

Sitting at a trendy fish-and-chip shop with Billy, he looked at me and said, 'You are pretty – but from certain angles you look incredibly plain.'

I was so crushed and felt so stupid. Memories of what that male model at the casting had said to me when I was 16 flashed through my head. Again, I knew I was cursed to be good but not good enough.

Twenty years later, Billy and I are friends. Over the years our paths have crossed a few times: once when I was doing a spoken-word tour in Australia and he was one venue ahead of me doing

Billy and I in Auckland the morning after the end of 1992's Big Day Out tour. We have remained friends to this day.

a solo tour, and another time when he was staying with Courtney Love a few streets away from where I lived in Los Angeles. It's always good to see him – he's a funny guy. And such a crazy-good musician. We were hanging out during the making of one of his albums and he had me bless and 'sage' the studio. The one time he was single, about seven years ago, he texted me: 'We should have made crazy Witch sex when we could have!' I was lying in bed with my boyfriend at the time. Our timing was always out. I have thought over the years to tell him how hurt I was about what he said to me that time we went out for dinner, but I decided I didn't want to make him feel bad. So, I just swallowed it … and I have made sure to try to tilt my head in an attractive angle in every photo taken of me since.

Back to being on the road with Def FX …

Sincere connections with other girls doing what I did were rare, and this forced me to seek out alternatives to the male-dominated industry I existed in. I found it in the New Age Goddess movement and Witchcraft, which was having a fresh run on the public scene in the writings of Starhawk, Z. Budapest and Ly de Angeles. Over the years, first driving in the tour van and then flying all over Australia's giant expanse and the long hauls between Australia and the USA, I devoured books like *The Way of the Goddess*, *The Spiral Dance* and writings on The Dianic Tradition. As soon as we checked into a hotel I would pull out my charm bag and set up my mobile altar of a candle, a crystal, a stick of incense and a bowl of water with a pinch of salt in it. As the years went on, people who were privy to my private obsession would gift me little statues of Goddesses, which I carried with me.

For as much as I didn't publicly proclaim to be a Witch, my Witchy interests came out in my song lyrics and, after an initial grunge phase, in the way that I dressed onstage, my costumes went all out rave magickal, culminating in a signature white jumpsuit with a pentagram over my stomach. This outfit had been created for me by local upcoming designer Mindy McTaggart. My bourgeoning Witchiness even influenced the co-founder of the band, who suggested we call an album *Majik,* in honour of the esoteric influences I was bringing to the band. It turned out to be our biggest seller.

Throughout Def's career I was primarily insecure. I looked to the co-founder for guidance and reassurance, yet as time went on, a rift developed between us. More than ever I felt I was being ganged up on by the boys. We would unite on stage and at rehearsals – but behind the scenes we would split. But there was one thing the tension behind the scenes could not get in the way of: my relationship with our fans. Def FX has the best fans. Our shows were a seething mass of dynamic energy. I would dive into the crowd and be held aloft on a sea of hands, passed up and across all the way to the back of the room and then all the way back up the front again.

Hecklers who cried 'Show us your tits!' were met with 'I will if you show me your dick! Wanna borrow my tweezers to find it?' And the crowd would roar with approval.

Sometimes, standing onstage as the familiar beats of one of our most popular songs started to kick in, I would literally see a shimmer of energy float up from the crowd. I could time it rushing towards me and then engulfing me, and my body would be electrified, nothing but goosebumps. I would throw back my head and howl – all the smothered screams of my childhood gushing out of me as the crowd screamed, echoing them back to me. It was fucking awesome. No matter how tired I was, how unsupported I felt, I would get onstage and everything made sense. It was a role so very different from the reclusive, shy girl of my childhood. But still not entirely, authentically me – it was more a persona I stepped into, to be what everyone wanted me to be. I loved it. And it was at these times that I knew who I was: I was 'Fiona from Def FX'.

But if I hung around with other performers and well-known people I still felt like the ugly duckling; the square peg in the round hole; the one who bluffed her way in because she was a Jill of all trades, master of none. Fiona from Def FX was a fake, someone who tried to make everyone think she was cool. And somehow she got away with it.

Eventually all that emotional screaming took its toll, not in the least because I was shrieking over an extremely loud band that was not concerned about my voice and my ability to hear myself. As I felt more ostracised by the guys, I sensed a lump of tension in my throat. I completely lost my voice and was diagnosed as having nodules on my vocal folds. Rather than surgery, I entered a treatment program to re-learn how to speak and sing using the muscles in my throat differently. I was taught how to shape my tongue to create a resonating chamber and project my voice loudly, without straining my vocal cords. To the management's credit, the band account paid for my time in therapy. Considering that I got only $50 a show when performing in front of hundreds (and even thousands) of people, it was the least our management could do.

It took three months, but the speech pathology worked and I was able to get back on the road. I never lost my voice again. And haven't in all the years since.

Reading back over band memories I am again struck by how negative so many of them are. I did have a lot of fun, though. I learned a lot. But, overall, the girl I was then doesn't resonate much with the person I am now. Except for Vipassana.

Considering that I lost my voice screaming, there was a time in the band that I chose not to speak for ten days. Behind the scenes, as much as I could, I was researching and practising alternative life choices and seeking to connect with a sense of peace and the Divine. I had picked up a brochure in a New Age store while on tour and read about Vipassana – a type of meditation centred around embracing Grand Silence.

To quote the brochure:

> *Vipassana, which means to see things as they really are, is one of India's most ancient techniques of meditation. It was taught in India more than 2500 years ago as a universal remedy for universal ills, ie: an Art of Living. The technique is taught at ten-day residential courses, during which participants learn the basics of the method, and practise sufficiently to experience its beneficial results. There are courses all over the world.*

Def FX had a break from touring, but not before I did an interview on *60 Minutes* about having tinnitus. The show was screening a special on the curse of constantly ringing ears – whether that be from a neck injury, medical condition or, in my case, repeated exposure to loud noise. I had tinnitus so bad it was like a thousand kettles screaming in my ears. Sometimes it sounded like a million china plates breaking on a metal floor (often still does). I've had tinnitus since 1994. I couldn't believe I was going to be on *60 Minutes* – it's such an iconic TV show. The interviewer, Jeff McMullen, was really nice and asked smart questions about being in a dumb, loud rock band, and how the tinnitus impacted my personal life. The most debilitating thing about tinnitus is that you never hear silence again. There is always this screaming, ringing sound in your ears. Even now as I type this. But I have learned to redefine what silence is to me. I refer to my screaming, ringing ears as 'the music of the spheres'. I imagine that it is the frequency emitted by planets, stars and solar systems as they whirl through the Universe. I breathe and have learned not to be angry about it. All these years later, during a 16-year Def FX reunion tour, our original bass player, Marty, said, 'Sorry, Fi, all those years you asked us to turn it down, we turned it up to fuck with you.' I wasn't angry. I just laughed a little and thought, So I wasn't just being a paranoid, grumpy girl back then – they really were turning it up.

All that being said, I wanted to do Vipassana and sit in my version of silence for ten days. After the interview with *60 Minutes* I jumped into a taxi and, with a cab charge provided by Channel 9, I rode all the way from Sydney to Blackheath in the Blue Mountains (that was a $200 ride. It was the 90s and money, well cab charges anyway, grew on trees).

The serene buildings of the retreat contrasted greatly with the wild venues and hotel rooms of the previous weeks' touring and I immediately felt a sense of peace and belonging. I was nervous because, now, I was just Fiona, not Fiona from Def FX. But the girls I was sharing a room with were friendly. There were four of us to a room, and we slept in bunks. Men and women were in separate buildings.

Dinner was simple vegetarian food. Everyone chatted quietly, introducing themselves and telling each other why they were there.

After dinner we gathered in the Main Hall and two monks instructed us in what Grand Silence is. And the retreat began.

As instructed by the monks, I was careful not to meet anyone's eyes or accidently speak as I headed to bed. As clustered together as we were, we all respected each other's commitment.

I was awoken by a monk ringing a gong at 4 am. I went to the Meditation Hall in the dark and with a beanie and two blankets thrown over me – it was freezing. I sat cross-legged on the right side of the hall. There were about 100 people – women on the right and men on the left. There were no decorations, no giant statues of Buddha, no smoking incense or flickering candles – just a dimly lit hall with a raised dais at one end. I focused on my breath flowing in and out of my nose and the sensation as it passed over my upper lip and the skin between it and my nose. This practice I had been taught in the initial session. It is called Anapana. That's all – for three hours. A gong sounded letting us know it was time to go to breakfast. My legs had gone to sleep so completely they were like two blocks of wood.

After a simple breakfast there was more Anapana meditation – this time when we gathered in the hall, a teacher at the front of the room pressed 'play' on a tape deck and we could hear the deep, mellifluous voice of S.N. Goenka, the modern proponent of Vipassana, who took it from India to the world. 'Equanimity, equanimity, equanimity' he would croon as my consciousness slipped below the horizon of my upper lip until 12 noon, when there was an hour break and we were allowed to stand in line at the door of a small room to speak to a teacher if we had a question. I didn't on my first day; I just went for a walk in the grounds. Then a light lunch, then more meditation. No dinner – just hot tea. We went to bed early and awoke with the gong – and the same routine continued for three days.

I was happy. It was really hard to sit in one place for hours and observe the flow of breath, but it was also simple, which I really liked. However, my monkey mind ultimately went crazy in these first three days, replaying conversations I had in the previous weeks, over and over again. My interview with Jeff McMullen played a billion times – I panicked that I should have said things better, smarter, more succinctly. I thought I was going out of my mind and considered talking to a teacher. But I didn't want to break my Grand Silence.

On the third day we were given Vipassana. We gathered in the hall and the teacher pressed 'play' on the tape machine. And now S.N. Goenka's voice crooned for two hours as he explained how to take this conscious awareness of energy and breath flowing over the upper lip – which by this time had become so huge in my own world, every hair was like a tree and they united in this giant forest balanced on my upper lip. My breath was the wind that swirled through the trees, rustling every follicle and dipping in and out of every pore.

Now I was to take this awareness and move it through my entire body – sweeping down and then sweeping up.

It sounds so simple, and yet it produced an extraordinarily complex sensation. My awareness swept through me like a broom whisking away blocks and pain – I alternatively felt like crying and laughing as Mr Goenka explained that what was happening was normal, that every experience was stored in our bodies and we could sweep our awareness through it all and clear blockages and attachments, cure any illness, cure any sadness. It was a way to live that allowed total freedom and clarity, and peace in the present moment.

After we had been given Vipassana we were free to go for a walk. What happened afterwards is still one of the most extraordinary and potent memories of my life.

Blackheath is a beautiful part of the mystical Blue Mountains and as I walked to the edge of the property, in a constant state of Vipassana, I did not feel the ground beneath my feet. I floated on a cloud of vibrating energy. I came to the edge of a cliff and to the base of a giant tree. My memory is that I ran up that tree like a leopard would – or maybe a ninja – effortlessly bounding up to a high thick branch before sitting on it, my legs stretched in front of me, my back against the trunk. I was merged with the tree; I couldn't fall out of it even if I tried. It wanted me there. It had invited me. Its branches had helped me up. I was there, buzzing and vibrating as the sun set in front of me. There were two mountains forming a V-shape and suddenly, from behind one of them, appeared a single parachute. Silhouetted against the setting sun it floated perfectly between the two mountains for what seemed like eternity before it floated to earth with the sun.

I was completely and utterly at one with the world and completely at peace. I had no past, no future, no flaws, no hurt – only love. But it was better than love. It was ultimate bliss.

I don't know how long the tree held me, but some time after it got dark I slid down and went to bed. I lay there constantly sweeping my attention up and down my body. I didn't really sleep that I'm aware of, but, at a point, the monk's gong chimed and I got up and went to the hall.

I continued in an ecstatic state for more days until one day I experienced a terrible pain as I swept my consciousness from my feet up to my head. It felt like there was a hard, wooden broomstick pushing up into the soft pallet of my mouth.

My monkey mind had calmed down and, for the most part, I had no thoughts. But this broomstick inside me was becoming an unbearable problem. I decided I needed to speak to a teacher.

On the sixth day of the retreat (I think) I stood at the door to the little room and was beckoned by a female monk sitting with a blanket around her. I sat on the floor and opened my mouth to speak. When the words left my throat I did not recognise my voice. But I managed to tell her what was happening every time I 'swept up'.

She said, 'Just sweep down.' I said, 'Is that okay to do?' She said, 'Yes.'

So that's what I did; I just swept down. Sending my awareness from the top of my head to the bottom of the soles of my feet and jumping straight back to my crown to send my awareness down again.

After a day of this, I did a test upward sweep and the pain was gone.

A huge problem had been solved with the simplest solution. It taught me that this is usually the best way to deal with all of life's problems, not just meditation problems. Keep it simple. Vipassana really is an 'Art of Living'.

It was day ten of the retreat and we gathered in the hall to break Grand Silence and head back out into the normal world.

I didn't want to leave; I didn't want to go back to being a rockstar, being *anything*. I just wanted to stay in the retreat for the rest of my life. Maybe I could be a monk and help with the gong in the mornings. I just wanted to go and visit my friend, the tree, and sit up there on its branch forever.

The monks announced Grand Silence was over and we could speak. One of the girls I had been sharing a room with was sitting next to me. She turned to me with a smile on her face and said, 'Well, you've been having a good time!' I could barely whisper, 'It's been amazing.' She said, 'Yes, I could tell! All night!' I said, 'What do you mean?' She said, 'You were talking away to all sorts of people in your sleep. And by the sound of it, the guy last night was pretty hot and you were having a fantastic time with him!' My face felt hot as I blushed. I said, 'I guess in not speaking all day my mind let out some words at night.' She said, 'Oh, yes, indeed, and it wasn't just you; it was the other girls, too. But you did the most!' We both laughed and she told me that she had attended multiple Vipassana retreats around the world and was familiar with the practice now. She said it got to a point where she didn't even sleep – she was just in a constant state of Vipassana during Grand Silence.

I vowed to attend Vipassana retreats around the world, too.

Getting into the taxi for the long drive back into the city, the everyday world assaulted me. The radio was so loud and shrill, the noise of the cars rushing by on the highway, the vibrating hum of the engine. It was all so invasive.

When I got back to where I was staying in the city I immediately sat and practised Vipassana. I felt calm again.

But the next day was band practice and, as I stood there in the rehearsal room, the thud and thwack of programmed drum beats felt like bazookas blasting holes in my aura.

I tried to keep up the practice but it made me too sensitive to noise, to life in general. I just wanted to run away back to the retreat.

That wasn't an option. So I stopped practising daily. However, over the twenty plus years since, I have searched out Vipassana sittings at various times of stress and need. Most recently, during my commercial pilot training in Santa Monica, California, I saw a notice in an organic grocery that there would be a group of Vipassana practitioners sitting in a community hall not far from where I was staying.

It always feels like coming home to see the familiar brochures laid out – they haven't changed in design over decades. It's good to silently nod to other practitioners as we enter the space and sit together and the person leading the group presses 'play' (this time on a laptop). S.N. Goenka's voice immediately soothes and captivates: 'Equanimity, equanimity, equanimity'.

Together we sweep away our problems, our illnesses, our grief, our joy, and exist together in peace.

'Unless you observe yourself you cannot come out of your problems.'
    S.N. Goenka

chapter four

THANK GOD YOU LOOK LIKE ME

*'Something inside ...
is keeping you alive.'*

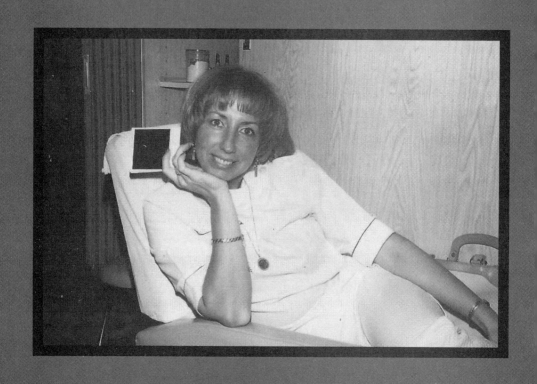

was living with Lydia, my dear girlfriend from the speed daze. She was flourishing in her nursing career and being a good, organised soul and had bought a lovely home in Leichardt. I was still in Def FX and on the road a lot, but it was great to have a home with her. Lydia gave me a sense of stability, which allowed me to look for my biological mother. I hadn't planned to, but my sister and brother are adopted, too, and they were getting married and planning to have families. The adoption laws had changed in Australia and identifying information was made available. My siblings wanted to know of any possible medical conditions that might affect their children. I wasn't concerned with that; I was just curious.

When I was given some identifying information about my blood parents and saw that my father's occupation was 'Used Car Salesman', this made perfect sense. I was an unhappy misfit as a child and convinced I was a dark mistake in the Universe. I must have been the accidental product of a back-seat tryst in an urban car lot. Just a random teaspoon of sperm and an egg gone awry.

I only had a desire to contact my mother, initially, and I created an elaborate ruse to find her. I pretended to be a university student and showed up at the Australian National

Library, where I scoured historical record-containing microfiche cards (this was in the days before the internet). Following a lead from the document provided by the Catholic Adoption Agency, I also unwittingly spoke to a man early in the search, who I would find out much later was actually my father.

It was the middle of a Def FX tour when I finally met my biological mother, Erika, in person in Queensland. I suggested we meet in a rented room at a bland hotel over the bus station at the Brisbane terminal. I don't know why I chose this strange, transient place. Maybe I wanted to be able to run away if it was terrible when I met her. I was so nervous the day of the meeting. I changed outfits ten times. I even went to Sussan clothing store and bought a conservative black shirt to wear. I wasn't sure what impression I should make. I was more nervous getting ready for this meeting than any time I had met a boy for a date.

Finally the time came – 6 pm – and there was a soft knock at the door. When I opened it the diminutive blonde woman in a bright red sweater clasped her hands in front of her heart and said, 'Thank God you look like me!'

I immediately felt claustrophobic at the sight of another human being who did indeed look like me.

The following years that Erika and I got to know each other were rocky. She had written on my original birth form that my father was a used-car salesman, to protect his identity. I was to find out that after she gave birth to me she went back and worked for him for 25 years, watching him fall in love with another woman and raise a family. I couldn't comprehend this sacrifice. I felt that I was the only tangible reminder of their love and I felt smothered. Often I felt inexplicable anger toward her. I would see her and she would comment on my behaviour: 'Oh, that's me in you', 'Oh, that's your father in you.' It would drive me nuts and I was rude and short with her. It was like I was a rebellious teenager all over again. I also would catch her just staring at me, which creeped me out. I learned my father wanted me aborted and had scheduled an appointment for her for the operation. It was only by chance that she went to another doctor, who was Catholic and who told her that 'Babies should live'. Erika went and lived with the doctor and his wife and their nine children and gave birth to me, immediately giving me up for adoption. She named me Vania Marie (which was superseded by Fiona Therese). I always thought it uncanny that both names were similar sounding.

For a time, I took on the name of Vania becuse I perceived it to be more exotic and with the qualities of the mysterious, compelling, magickal person I aspired to be. But eventually I went back to Fiona, and gradually Erika and I became friends.

And I discovered she is a bird charmer. The first time I witnessed it I couldn't quite believe it. Wild birds hopped after her like she was a bird magnet. When we met she lived in a classic Queenslander house on stilts. Back then I was still nervous around her and, during one visit, I was on my best behaviour, sitting up straight with my legs crossed at the kitchen table, and I watched her crouch at the top of her long steps and say, 'Here Charlie!' I peeked over her shoulder and I could see a wild magpie hopping up the stairs, one by one, toward her, cocking its head as it listened to her voice. She got up and walked inside and the bird came right inside with her! It was the strangest thing. It just followed her around like a dog. She left the door open and after an hour or so it hopped to the step and flew away.

I've watched my mother hand-feed wild birds, like Kookaburras, and now, in her small Brisbane apartment, she has a balcony where she lays out strips of meat for them every day.

Erika is a very solitary person, I have come to learn. And a survivor. The year we met she was coming out of a bankruptcy that happened when a man she eventually married took her to the cleaners. She started her own beauty business in Brisbane and went on to win various small-business awards and cultivate a devoted group of clients. She would often be booked out two years in advance. After fifteen years of a packed schedule, she has downscaled her business to enjoy a kind of 'retirement'. But she will always want to spend time with her 'ladies' at the salon, and still works three days a week.

In her Sensational Seventies (as she calls it!) she is single and likes to relax alone watching TV and enjoying a glass of 'champies' (champagne, in her words) and enjoying brunch with the family at the local RSL club on Sundays (her sister and niece and nephews live nearby).

But I don't want to end up like Erika. I don't want to be that alone. But some similarities in our lives are uncanny. For example, my mother had a serious motorbike accident in her 42nd year and her foot was pretty much torn off and surgically reconnected. She never regained her full mobility. In my 42nd year I jumped out of an aeroplane, stepped in a gopher hole on landing my parachute, and broke my ankle on the same leg. Luckily I had a good surgeon and regained full mobility, albeit with an ankle held together by more titanium than bone.

But these synchronicities and parallel patterns only compel me to ensure, by hook or by crook, that I will not be watching TV in bed, drinking champagne, when I'm 70.

I also got to know my father over two meetings. His family kept us apart, possibly concerned that I would come after money. They are very wealthy. But I decided if I had inherited anything from my father it would be his ability to make my own money and I haughtily said to myself and my biological mother, when she suggested it would be nice if my biological father gave me some support, that I would make my own fortune. Looking back, I didn't inherit his gift with money. But I did inherit his gift for survival.

This is my father …

Surrounded by horror, then beauty

September 16 2002

Original article published by Sydney Morning Herald

George Gabriel Korner, Businessman 1918–2002

A man known to many as the creator of the modern-day beauty business in Sydney, Hungarian-born George Gabriel Korner, survived both a Nazi slave labour battalion and the Russian front in winter to bring 'beauty to Australia'.

George was brought up in a cultured household in the days of the Austro-Hungarian Empire. His father, Dr Eugene Korner, was a lawyer trained in the Napoleonic code and a bridge master, and his mother, Johanna, the original Madame Korner, a leader in the beauty industry in Europe.

George developed his business around the credo that there was no such person as an ugly woman, only women who had neglected themselves. The family's cosmetics business, which would eventually become central to his life and livelihood, meant that George, even as a youngster, was surrounded – as he would be all his life – by beautiful women.

George, a Jew who celebrated his 20th birthday on the day of Kristalnacht, was forced into a Nazi slave labour battalion when Hungary joined the Axis powers.

The men of his battalion were marched to the Russian front as human minesweepers and cannon fodder. The survivors reached the suburbs of Moscow in the winter before being abandoned by the retreating Nazi army.

George survived typhus, typhoid, a severe wound to his leg, shrapnel in his head and being declared dead and loaded on to a wagon with corpses. He was rescued when a friend noticed he was still breathing.

Abandoned without food, winter clothing or equipment, the remnants of the battalion set out for Budapest on foot. Trudging homeward, they found in a snowbank a box of butter which had fallen from a vehicle. Labelled 'A gift from the people of New

George Korner presents a student of his beauty therapy college with her graduation certificate.

Zealand to the gallant people of Russia', the box sustained the group for some time. George said later it was the best food he had ever tasted and he resolved to see its country of origin one day.

Only three of the 1000-strong battalion survived the long walk. All ended up in Australia, remained friends and prospered.

George later declared: 'After what we'd been through in the war we could do anything here. For us, even being in an Australian jail would have seemed a picnic. We never thought we'd live another day, let alone be able to look forward to warmth and a meal.'

After the war, George lived in Paris with his parents and sister Magda, who also later came to Australia. With the help of a strict exercise campaign and his inimitable spirit, he acquired a reputation as a playboy.

It was on holidays in the south of France that he learned to scuba dive – then a very new sport which had grown out of wartime underwater breathing equipment developments, and the key to his coming to Australia. He first visited for a spearfishing contest at the end of 1950 and, fearing further unrest in Europe, he later brought out his parents, his sister and her children.

On arrival in Sydney, George was chastised by the surf patrol on Bondi beach for wearing a European-style brief leopard skin swimsuit. He was ordered to cover up with a pair of baggy, white boxer-style shorts.

He also astounded the locals by shooting, with a spear gun, a two-metre shark in the surf and pulling it ashore. Ordered to remove the shark from the beach, he was forced to negotiate with a taxi driver to have it transported to the boarding house in which he was living at Rushcutters Bay.

The boarding house owner, also unimpressed, made him dispose of the catch.

George's first job in Sydney was as a labourer in the Dalgety wool stores. While there he devised a grading system which continued to be used well into the 1980s.

He also devised a business around the waste trimmings from sheepskins sent to Europe. He rented a tanning plant in the inner-western suburbs on weekends and loaded the trimmings into the plant's tanning vats. He skimmed the wool off the acid bath and baled it for sale to foreign markets.

His next project involved Australian lanolin, also a by-product of wool. At the time, the wool scouring companies almost gave away the raw lanolin to British processors for reshipment back to Australia as a women's skin care product at 10 shillings a jar. Knowing he could refine the lanolin in Sydney and sell it for half the price, George set up in business.

However his product, labelled 'Genuine Australian Lanolin', didn't sell without the expensive price tag. George solved the problem by lifting the price to 15 shillings. The company he set up to manufacture lanolin eventually became part of the core of Marrickville Holdings, the margarine manufacturer and, at one stage, one of Australia's major manufacturing companies.

With the arrival of his parents and sister, George combined his panache and knowledge of chemistry with the expertise of his mother and sister and began the task of establishing the Madame Korner chain of skin care salons in Sydney and the first beauty therapy training college in Australia.

Although European women had long been aware of the

secrets of good beauty treatment, skin care in Australia at the
time was elementary and didn't take account of the damage
the harsh climate wreaks on fair complexions. Through his
work, George revolutionised the way Australian women, and
eventually men, look after their skin.

By researching and creating new products and promoting
the benefits of healthy skin care, he was instrumental in making
people aware of the importance of caring for themselves from an
early age.

With newspaper articles and radio and TV appearances,
he soon became a household name throughout Australia. He
opened more salons in Sydney, Melbourne, Adelaide and
Hobart and the Madame Korner name became the benchmark
for skin care and beauty therapy training.

At 51, with his chain of salons already successful, he married
a student beautician, Judit Botta, who had fled Hungary in
1956 and was almost 30 years his junior. Together, they raised
three daughters: Jessica, Rebecca and Olivia.

George's legacy in caring for people and teaching will be
carried on by his wife and three daughters in the Madame
Korner chain of salons and beauty schools.

So, I am the daughter of a Holocaust-surviving, dashing, beauty businessman, and an attractive German Lutheran girl, who is a top beautician and bird charmer … among other things. I have a genetic World War II raging inside me. It explains a lot of things.

When my father met my mother, he was 44 and she was 20. He was the head of a beauty empire and her family had also migrated to Australia after the war. She had gone to the top beauty school of the day to train as a beautician. My father was tall, dark and handsome. I remember the day I uncovered that the famous George Korner was my father: I had taken a train into Sydney and had stood outside his beauty empire 'Madame Korner', which was housed in the Hilton Hotel. There was a giant, framed black-and-white poster featuring a spiral staircase on which young girls were seated, wrapped only in white towels. At the foot of the staircase stood a debonair man in an immaculate black suit with his hand in one pocket. The caption said, 'God created Woman … and George Korner made her beautiful.'

I contemplated what would have happened if I had got off the train one stop later, back when I was sixteen, and had gone to Madame Korner's school of beauty instead of June Dally-Watkins'. So near yet so far.

If I had gone to Madame Korner's back then, my mother would have been my teacher in the deportment course. She was one of the company's top beauticians and headed their school curriculum. We look so similar it would have been immediately noticeable.

When I stood looking at that poster, however, I felt intimidated and unworthy. I was the sad teenager who left home at 14 and lived on the streets for a time. To see that I was heir to something glamorous and successful just made me feel like a dark, ugly secret – an even darker mistake in the Universe. Well, that's how I made myself feel. Truth be told, I was a secret. My German grandparents died never knowing their eldest daughter had a child. Erika didn't tell anyone she got pregnant in that first year she went to the big city.

At least I could take solace in knowing that I was not the

product of an affair. My father told me in the first of our two meetings: 'I loved your mother when you were conceived.'

My mother has told me about the night I was conceived. She and George had gone camping at Jervis Bay, on the southern NSW coast. He had gone out fishing in a little boat. The sun had set and it was very dark. My mother was worried that George was lost at sea. She stood under a light at the end of the pier, looking into the blackness, and then she saw him emerge from the dark. She said when he climbed out of the boat and hugged her she knew she loved him.

They went back to the campsite and made love by the fire, and my life started.

But George could never marry Erika. He was a Jew and she was a German, and only a little over 20 years had passed since the war. It was all too close to the bone. My father's sister still had a concentration camp number tattooed on her wrist.

A few years after my birth my father married another beauty student, a lovely Hungarian girl named Judit. She gave birth to my half-sisters Olivia, Rebecca and Jessica. I love being able to say, now, that Judi and I are close friends, and I went to my sister Rebecca's wedding in Paris. Jessica is super sweet. I am very close to Olivia, my wild and beautiful sister, and we get together whenever I am in Sydney. Oli's three gorgeous daughters, Chloe, Poppy and Ruby, are like my own nieces. Judi is an extremely cool woman and I love spending time with her. She tells me to call her 'Love Mother', not 'Step Mother'. I adore her. But for over a decade a meddlesome cousin, who was jockeying his position of favour with my father by using the inconvenient fact that I existed, as leverage, kept me from knowing Judi and my sisters.

My cousin has passed now. I sometimes wonder what would have happened if he had not kept us all apart. Judi says, 'You should have been at Friday night Shabbat with us. I would ask about you but your cousin always said you didn't want to join us.' If only I had known. I would have loved to be there.

From a certain angle, you could look at my humble upbringing in suburban Sydney juxtaposed with the glamorous eastern suburbs city life of my blood family and think that I was missing out. But I have learned that every family has their challenges no matter what their social status. I am grateful to be close to my blood family now. The parents I grew up with still aren't that happy with me though! Having known them for half a century, now, I have decided to accept that maybe I will never be good enough for them. And that's okay. It's more important that I'm good enough for me. My upbringing largely made me the person I am today, so in a sense I could consider myself grateful for having such a painful childhood – it gave me a point of reference to grow from and choose to create a different, happier life for myself; it sparked in me a desire to escape … but that also became a desire to explore and experience different things.

I now live, literally, on the other side of the world to Australia. But, at times I have considered if one day my life will come full circle and I will move back. I miss my awesome sister Samantha and my cool train-driver brother Greg (who could also give up his day job to be a comedian, he has the most acerbic wit!), and his lovely wife, Marie, as well as all my wonderful nieces and nephews: Julia, Caity, Luke and Jason, Mitchell and Ben. I love spending time with them all so much when I am back in Australia – watching my nephews Luke, Ben and Mitchell kill it in indoor cricket, soccer and the footy, and Caity twirling like a fairy princess in her jazz-ballet performances. I'm so proud of Jason, my first nephew, at seventeen so handsome and working his first job as an apprentice butcher at a fancy supplier in Surry Hills. And Julia, my first niece, so grown up at fifteen and cool with her purple hair, Audrey Hepburn t-shirts and Doc Marten boots, learning Korean not because it's required at school but because she thinks it's interesting. But like the Universe, forever expanding, I think I will continue to expand also – moving onward and outward – but I will always love visiting the amazing country of my birth.

chapter five

FIONA THE HOT WITCH

'Magick, magick –
I'll be your magick …'

FIONA HORNE HOT NUDE PICTORIAL

PLAYBOY

AUSTRALIAN EDITION

INTERVIEW:
THE DEVIL INSIDE
MIKE TYSON

ANOTHER, SIR?
THE PERFECT
MARTINI REVEALED

PARTY AT THE
PLAYBOY CLUB

COLLEGE
GIRLS
UNCOVERED

FROM DEF-FX TO WITCH AND BEYOND . . .

FIONA HORNE

MYTH, MAGICK & MYSTERY

WitchCraft

FEBRUARY/MARCH 2001 #18
$4.95 (inc GST)
NZ $7.95 (inc GST)

JANET &
STEWART
FARRAR
Modern Wicca's most
famous Witches

CASSANDRA
CARTER
Keeper of Celtic Wisecraft

How to commune with
SPIRIT GUIDES

JUST-ADD-WATER
Spells for health,
prosperity and friendship

CURSING & HEXING
Should you or shouldn't you?

THE MAGICK WITHIN
Discover how to unlock your power

EXCLUSIVE EXTRACT
From Fiona Horne's latest book

don't want to do it anymore.'

'What? The band?'

'Yes.'

'Is there anything we can talk about?'

'No.'

He hung up.

That was the transcript from the murder of my band by its co-founder.

The brutal and abrupt nature of Def FX breaking up in our seventh year together was insanely traumatic for me. For all my growing fascination and obsession with the magickal and psychic world, I was pretty much blindsided by this act of betrayal. For three months I floundered, unable to sleep and pacing the streets of Melbourne at night going nowhere in particular. I would say over and over in my head 'I will rise like a phoenix from the flames' not knowing how I would do it. The band had not been managed well, or honestly, and I had no money. It was April 1997 – I had been working 24/7 for seven years as Fiona from Def FX and I was handing in an unemployment benefits form at the social security office the same week I was featured in Australia's WHO Weekly, as one of Australia's 'Best Dressed

Celebrities of 1996', for my quirky style.

A person standing in the dole queue behind me said, 'But you're Fiona Horne, what are you doing here?'

I realised if I handed in that form I would be telling the Universe that, after all my hard work, I was only ever going to be worth $300 a fortnight. I would be letting my father's words, 'You will always fail at everything you do', win. I didn't hand in the form and left the dole office.

I was grateful that person spoke to me. Her name is Wendy Rule – at the time a gifted songwriter and performer … and Witch, who would go on to carve a unique, magickal niche, internationally, as a celebrated Pagan musician and real-life Goddess. We ultimately became great friends in magick and the physical world, performing together onstage at special events … and decades later we are still friends.

Not long after meeting Wendy at the dole office, I reached out and got an introduction to a publisher, courtesy of a good friend in radio at the time, Helen Razer. Her book *Three Beers and a Chinese Meal*, co-authored with her hit breakfast-radio show co-host, Mikey Robins, was a bestseller. She was gunning for me that I should tell some of my rock 'n' roll tales. I got a book deal with the same publisher, Random House. The publisher, Jane Palfreyman, said, 'A rock star writing a book about Witchcraft – that should sell a few copies!' And it did – it became a bestseller. So, ultimately, the end of the band launched me on the next path of survival, writing books about Witchcraft and becoming an international poster girl for the Craft for the next ten years.

A process and undertaking that was largely made up as I

"I'VE HAD A FULL ON LIFE ALREADY," SAYS HORNE, AT HOME WITH A FEW OF HER FAVOURITE THINGS "BUT I PLAN TO BE EXACTLY LIKE THIS WHEN I'M 80 OR 90."

WHO Weekly spread, as one of Australia's 'Best Dressed Celebrities of 1996'.

went along – maybe that was the magic of it. But underneath something felt unauthentic. I could talk the talk – I knew so much theory after seven years of behind-the-scenes research and secret rituals during Def FX, I could write reams on paper – but did I feel it? Did I believe it? As something so personal played out on the world stage I was often left feeling as if I was acting up to people's expectations rather than experiencing a profound spiritual connection to anything myself.

I went out and got my first shot of Botox – I wanted to erase the axe wound of a frown between my eyebrows, from the seven years in Def FX.

Then I posed for Australian *Playboy*. I was paid good money and I chose a female photographer and an all-women team for the shoot. I did it to celebrate the life of infamous Witch and artist, Rosaleen Norton.

I had to pinch myself that ugly me was going to be in *Playboy*. I remember when I was little, my brother and me reaching under Dad's side of the bed to find his stash of *Playboy* magazines when he and Mum were out. Now here I was being tortured – having my breasts taped up so they weren't droopy (all that gaffa tape would have been a nightmare to retouch in the days before Photoshop) and endless cubes of ice applied to my sensitive nipples to make them hard. My favourite memories of the shoot are having a giant snake slither over me at night in the front yard of a Double Bay mansion and swimming with turtles in a plastic wading pool lined with black plastic, in the photographer's city studio. Sitting naked in the front window of the Piccolo Bar in Kings Cross with my wrists handcuffed was less fun because of the passersby staring in. This shot was done to recreate an actual time in Rosaleen's young life when she was a nude model in the artist's studio above that very coffee shop. She would model and then wander down the spiral staircase, still naked, to the coffee shop below and order a latte. Or however they served coffee back in the 50s.

Witches have always been exhibitionists.

Me and my lovely gay boyfriend Matt Thomas – living the life together in the 90s – we still enjoy a wonderful friendship today.

I had the pleasure of joining Matti's band, The Mavis's, onstage, jamming on the number one hit song he wrote about our relationship, 'Cry'.

I made the move to Melbourne after the end of Def FX, for a sweet guy I fell in love with, Matt, from The Mavis's. Def FX's last tour happened to be with them. Matt was gay but the desire for a relationship together overcame his natural proclivities and we had an exciting, sangria-soaked time together, travelling to Thailand and being a bit of a celebrity couple. We lived in a two-room apartment above a petrol station on the corner of Brunswick St in Fitzroy. The walls were decorated with quirky art-deco stuff – all Matti's taste. I remember watching *Recovery* on TV and being so surprised that the host, Dylan, was auctioning a giant nude picture of me with a metal spike through my lip and metal armour on my arm, as originally published in *(not only) Black + White* magazine. It was bought for $2000. I was still deeply depressed about the end of Def FX. I felt so lost. But I was writing my book. At a little desk sandwiched between the wardrobe and the window. My view was of a passionfruit vine clustered over the wood paling fence next door. I was fascinated by the intricate purple and white flowers and I would spend hours gazing at them when I had writer's block.

Matti and I had some wonderful times, and great sex, too, once we worked out how to do it. But ultimately, he was gay and we were young and fighting a lot. We parted as friends and are still friends to this day. His sister Beki is one of my very closest friends. He has a beautiful husband, Byron, and I love seeing them so happy together and working on cool music projects.

By 1999 I had two bestselling Witchy books and a lot of media, radio and television exposure as a guest and hosting my own shows/segments. I was busy, had great friends and felt more secure than I had for a long time.

I moved from grungy Fitzroy to trendy St Kilda and, during a celebrity modeling event for Wella hair products, I met a girl backstage, Krista Vendy, who was starring on the soap *Neighbours*. Years after we would always laugh about how I went up to her said, 'I've been sitting on the other side of the room looking at you and thinking "Who is the blonde with the lovely long legs?"'

We became best friends and shared a glamorous apartment. We had good-looking boyfriends and went to the races and other high-profile social events together, where we were photographed. We were always in the papers and the magazines, together and individually. We were living the dream! And having so much fun. It was an amazing time and the perfect antidote to all the grief of Def FX breaking up the way it had. I loved having a home with her and not being on the road all the time. I could ride my pushbike just around the corner to Triple M radio station, where I had my own Sunday night national Aussie music show *Home Grown*. I was also recording their *Planet Rock* Top 40 national rock countdown.

Our home ended up being the location for quite a few fun telecasts and photoshoots.

When I got a job as music reporter for Network Ten's *Ground Zero*, I had people like Melissa Etheridge over to my house for lunch – she loved playing with my snake, Lulu! Such a cool lady. But the strangest shoot was when Don Burke from *Burke's Backyard* came over and interviewed me for his hugely popular show. He was the most vulgar man I've ever met! I think it's so scorched in my memory because he was so squeaky clean on TV – but off screen he had a dirty mouth and an even dirtier mind. I remember I couldn't breathe when he said, 'You know you keep getting a face lift and eventually you'll have a beard just like us fellas.'

If you want to see my fabled appearance on *Burke's Backyard* and *Celebrity Who Wants to be a Millionaire*, my friend Rob Wilmshurst kindly made a YouTube channel that has almost every TV appearance I've ever made! You can see it by going to my website: fionahorne.com

In addition to having my own radio shows on Triple M I was groomed to be the Nine Network's darling, with a great management team working hard for me – Terry Blamey and Melissa LeGear. I scored my own prime-time show called *Party* on Channel 9. I owe so much of my success during this time to Terry and Melissa's hard work and passion – not only sourcing opportunities for me but also following up all the leads I was getting while I ran around being a society gal, too.

I gained huge notoriety for going to the Logies bra-less, wearing only a necktie for a top and a big floppy hat courtesy of new, edgy designer Princess Highway.

It was all harmless and a lot of fun.

I was dating a lovely footballer named Clint. It was time for his annual trip away at the end of the season with the team. I gave him a bag of condoms and said, 'Go and have a good time. If you have a good story tell me about it. If I don't need to know then don't tell me, and don't bring me back any surprises.'

He went to Mykonos and came back with a story about a girl he shagged in an alleyway … who was from Adelaide. I said, 'God you went all the way to Greece to shag a chick from Adelaide?'

I was attempting to be open-minded and cool, but in fact I was micro-managing the world so that it couldn't hurt me and betray me again. I always felt like I was one step away from a disaster. But really, when I look back, everything was great.

My personal Witchcraft at this time was enjoyable. I loved my snakes, which sometimes got out and freaked Krista out. I remember the time she called a snake handler she knew from her TV show because Sebastian, my largest snake – a five-foot long, dark-green NSW coastal carpet python – had got out and hidden behind the stove.

I especially loved snakes because, to me, they represented the Goddess – the Pagan Goddess that existed in the Garden of Eden before Adam and Eve arrived. Lulu, in particular, was not my pet; she was my Familiar – my magickal partner, who I would include in all my rituals and spells. She would sit contentedly around my neck while I lit candles and burned incense. I carefully collected the skins my snakes shed to use in spells and good-luck charms. When I needed a new TV show or radio gig I would crumble some of the skins into the ocean and a new job would come flowing in the next day.

Life in Melbourne was great – including being paid $2000 to walk into a Crown Casino nightclub. The night was called 'Horny Thursdays'. I just had to show up with some friends and request a couple of songs from the DJ.

I was everywhere and yet, in my heart, it didn't feel like it was good enough. I didn't know where I should go or what I should do. I also felt I was being hit by the tall-poppy syndrome. Then I met Tom Jones and he planted a seed that I should move to Los Angeles.

I met Tom when I interviewed him live for a TV show I was music reporter on. His comeback song 'Sex Bomb' was Number 1 on the charts and he was performing sold-out shows in arenas all around the country. I was granted the only live interview. I had recently interviewed Britney Spears in Japan and she had confessed to me that her favourite position was 'on top'. That interview went viral on Reuters. I was a hot ticket. I had been flown from my Melbourne home to do this interview at the Ritz Carlton in Double Bay, Sydney. But all I could think about was the next day. I was planning to go to Hepburn Spa mineral springs outside of Melbourne, with my girlfriends, for a much-needed rest. I wanted to get back home. Tom and I were seated together on the rooftop of the Ritz. I was wearing an ear piece and my producer was feeding me questions through it. Tom and I were holding smoking cigars and I was pouring him cognac (as I was directed to) and asking him questions about when 'he likes to do it' (again being directed by the producer's voice in my ear). When I said this, Tom raised an eyebrow and looked at me in a cheeky way and asked, 'What do you mean?' My producer was silent. I said, 'You know, gettin' jiggy with it!' (as the popular Will Smith song at the time went). All of a sudden my producer was screaming in my ear: 'No! No! We're a family show!' I ad-libbed: 'Tom, how about we hear some of your hit song?' And Tom obliged singing 'Sex Bomb' to the break.

Ugh – I was in trouble. After the interview Tom was trying to flirt with me and asked me what I was doing after the interview, which, under other circumstances would have been flattering, but my producer was telling me I had just lost my job – and hers. As soon as I could, I got out of there and was on a plane back to Melbourne. I did eventually lose my job but it wasn't until after another scandal.

Tom was spending a month touring around Australia and when he got to Melbourne his record company gave me two tickets to his show. I took my roomie, Krista, and we had prime seats. As I looked at this man onstage and the tens of thousands of screaming fans he held in the palm of his hand, I realised I was pretty lucky to get the one live interview with him. Even if it had been an outrage. Why was it an outrage? Tom was married, but we didn't know that. I don't think my producer researched that. Tom was a self-confessed ladies' man; his exploits were well documented, but we didn't know he had been married to the same woman since he was sixteen – a woman who lived in Los Angeles and never traveled with him or was seen in public. Because my interview was in prime time, the censorship board complained that what I implied was lewd and inappropriate.

Anyway, the concert ended and I turned to my roomie and said, 'We have backstage passes. We should probably go and say "thank you" for the concert.' So we headed back and were greeted by record company execs and invited to wait in the green room.

We hung around sipping wine for an hour, but there was no sign of Tom. My roomie and I were getting tired and wanted to leave, so I said to the record exec, 'Could you please let Tom know that Fiona, the girl who interviewed him on TV, is here and would like to thank him for the concert?'

He scurried off and seconds later I heard a booming voice; 'FIONA LUV!' And Tom was wrapping me in a bear hug. I didn't leave his side for two weeks.

I fell head over heels for Tom, and he appeared to fall for me, too. Yes, he was married. But he assured me that he and his wife had 'an arrangement' and as long as he didn't flaunt a girlfriend in Los Angeles, where she lived, he could do what he wanted. I was so swept up in it all and his relationships with many women had been so well documented that it honestly didn't occur to me that there was anything untoward about sleeping with a married man. Nothing about Tom suggested 'married'.

We ended up staying together back at the Ritz Carlton in Double Bay. Our usual routine would be that he would perform at another sold-out arena, then we would go and have a huge dinner with assorted hangers-on and other celebrities, and then stay up all night drinking Remy XO and black coffee and smoking cigars. Then we would go to bed at 7 am and wake up at 4 pm to coffee and club sandwiches. We would sit there in our robes and rev up for another evening. This also involved lots of cuddles and Tom was a very generous lover – in every way! He had a huge voice, a huge heart … a huge everything, actually! He would say, 'Oh Fiona, love, I wish I'd met you ten years ago.' And I would say, 'Tom, really, it's no problem – you're amazing!' But we kept our cuddles to before the show, when he had lots of energy … when we got back to the hotel at the end of the long nights, all we wanted to do was pass out!

It was my job to retrieve the papers from under the door and, on this particular day when I picked up the *Sydney Morning Herald*, I nearly threw up. The headline read 'Tom's Bewitched' and there was a picture of me leaving a hotel with Tom. The story said that I had been having an affair with him since the TV interview (not true by two weeks) and that I had used Magic to bewitch him away from his wife.

I actually think the opposite was true; he had bewitched me.

He was from Wales and told me his grandmother was a Witch – I think she taught him some tricks. When Tom's tour came to an end I gave him a lucky charm I had made: it featured a genuine four-leaf clover I had found, a piece of amber, and the bone from a fox penis (said to guarantee virility). I put all this in a little sandalwood box and wrapped a bow around it. He loved it.

He said if I ever came to LA he would introduce me to the right people and I could work on being the World's Favourite Witch – not just Australia's. It definitely set the cogs in my brain whirring.

Then I met another man who planted a second LA seed: Marilyn Manson. His band was touring Australia on the Big Day Out and I scored an interview with him for my radio show on Triple M. I had read he liked snakes, so I decided to take my little Familiar, Lulu, in with me. She was a desert python, indigenous to the Northern Territory and a sweet one-and-a-half feet long. She was the loveliest snake. I used to set her in between my boobs and she would curl around my bra and sit there in my t-shirt with her little head poking out.

Mid-interview with Manson and guitarist John 5, Lulu stuck her head out and caught Manson's eye. When he realised I was a *Playboy* cover girl, that also got his attention. I had done my feature spread a few months before and I guess he had seen a copy. Manson said he really liked my make-up on the cover. I had eyes done a bit like Daryl Hannah's in *Blade Runner* – black eyeshadow painted like a tilted mask. And I had long black talons for fingernails. *Playboy* has never done a cover like it before or since. I was proud of the shoot. At that time in my life I considered nudity just another selling tool, and because I was rebuilding my life from the end of Def FX I said yes to almost everything. I also justified it by looking to other Aussie girls who had posed for *Playboy*, including the girl from my first modeling casting – supermodel Elle Macpherson. And my dear girlfriend Dannii Minogue. I decided I was in good company and it was an empowering thing to do. But still I was relentlessly cruel to myself. I would viciously squeeze my thighs in front of the mirror and claim I had ugly cellulite. These fits of self-hatred had punctuated my teen and adult life. I even punched myself in the face once after a Def FX show, giving myself a black eye.

Doing *Playboy* subverted some of that induced self-hatred – and it piqued Manson's interest. He invited me to the band's show the next night and I went. He was glorious on stage. This was during the release of the band's second album *Antichrist Superstar* and his performance was grotesquely beautiful. We hung out after the show and I was privy to Manson and John 5's wild and wacky ways. They had rigged up John 5's hotel room with a camera that looked like an alarm clock and John 5 would go downstairs and pick out an adoring young fan and invite her up with the promise to meet Manson. He would take the girl to the room while Manson watched the proceedings on the TV in his suite at the end of the hall. But interestingly, Manson didn't want any of it. His eyes were hurting and he wasn't happy that his eye doctor wasn't on the road with him as usual. The thick contact lenses he wore, to give his face a demonic look, were scratching his cornea and he didn't know what to do to stop the pain – and he didn't want to take them out.

When I was in the room with Manson he made a point of turning his back to the TV and only focusing on talking to me.

In the midst of all this rock 'n' roll excess Manson was charming and kept refilling my wine glass and offering me fruit and cheese from a platter.

I decided to leave at 3 am.

The next day I missed a call from 'Brian'. I called back and it was Manson inviting me to a movie that night. His friend Gus Van Sant had directed a remake of *Psycho* and he wanted to take me. I went, and we actually had a really nice night. Away from the 'Manson' persona he was really sweet. After the movie we went to play video games at the casino, and a few other band members joined us. After about an hour I realised Manson was gone. John 5 told me he wasn't feeling well and had returned to his room. I decided to leave.

The next day I got another call from 'Brian', who apologised profusely. He told me he was sorry he left so abruptly, but he really was ill and was seeing a doctor. The band were leaving to play Adelaide the next day and he said it was really nice meeting me. I said it was really nice meeting him, too. I was also really glad I hadn't crossed a physical line with him because I'd put it together that he had a girlfriend, the eventual star of *Charmed*, Rose McGowan. In fact, the two of them had just been to the MTV Awards that year, where she had worn that infamous, invisible black-mesh dress. She had arrived with him in Australia, first stop Brisbane, but they had a huge fight and she went back to LA. Years later Rose and I became friends when she was starring in a Quentin Tarantino movie that a friend of mine was working on. I never mentioned my 'Brian' experience. Nothing really happened. And as far as I knew he had been faithful to her – unless being a voyeur could be considered unfaithful.

In the aftermath of that meeting, the second seed of my

Pictures from my youngest years growing up in Illawong – that's my brother Greg in front of the Christmas tree with me.

Clockwise from top left: Trying to model at 15 and feeling terribly uncomfortable – the photographer wanted me to look like Brooke Shields in *Pretty Baby*; Rocking out on stage at The Hopetoun Hotel with The Mothers, at 21 ; 'E-ing' off my head, sitting on my bed in my beachside squat, at age 23.

Clockwise from top left: My biological mother, Erika, and I the night we met for the first time; I am standing next to Dr Nolan – the man that made sure I wasn't put in a bucket. Erika and the doctor's wife are to my right; I felt like I was meeting the Goddess, when I met my Aunt Magda - the original Madame Korner - she had incredible skin and was such a glamorous woman; George Korner loved the ocean – I inherited that trait from him.

Clockwise from top left: Loving the Livid crowd in Def FX (Photo: Tony Mott); the *Ritual Eternal* album shoot, sporting my new labrette piercing after Vipassana – symbolic of the ten days I did not speak; Onstage during Def FX's Majik album era, 1996; Eventually I got comfortable being photographed – even with a spike in my lip.

Clockwise from top left: My teen crush, Paul Stanley of KISS the night I gave him my book; I interviewed Britney in Japan – we hung out –she's so sweet!; My favourite Witch in the world, Christian Day; Elle Macpherson and I at the Logies, years after we met at a Clearasil commercial casting – she remembered!; Gwen and I had fun touring with our bands together.

Clockwise from top left: Def FX 15-year reunion tour poster; 16-year reunion poster!; Marty Basha, our original bassist, and me having too much fun back onstage together (photo Dean Perkins); Rocking hard in 2013 at The Gov, Adelaide, on our national reunion tour (photo: A & K Photography).

Clockwise from top left: Girlfriends are the best! My island BFF, Haley Olson and I about to hit the ocean at home; My favourite mountain woman, Sarah Lassez and I, at her beautiful Lake Arrowhead home; Fifi, my beloved, rescued Crucian mutt enjoying an island sunset with me; Decades of divine friendship with beautiful Dannii – her talented son took this lovely photo!; My sweet Beki Colada – she let me sleep in her bed and eat from her fridge all year during flight school in Los Angeles.

Top row left to right: My new career as an aviation Marketing Manager in 2015; Successfully completed the BushAir bush flying course in South Africa, 2016.

Mid row left to right: First Haiti mission 2017, transporting 350 laying chicks; Second mission delivered school supplies and tools.

Bottom row: I love flying turbine multi-engine planes – here on St Kitts with the fast, manoeuvrable Beech99.

Me and my bestie, Beki, from The Mavis's (and Nic from the band)
meet our idols, KISS.

relocation to LA took hold. I had never mingled with celebrities
simply as Fiona Horne – it had always been 'Fiona from Def FX'.
Now I was seeing the world as a stage I could possibly perform on
solo – as the World's Favourite Witch.

What sealed the deal for me was meeting the God of Thunder
and Rock 'n' Roll, Gene Simmons.

Growing up I was a massive KISS fan. I was a member of the
KISS Army. I had a *Dynasty* poster above my bed under the bunk
I shared with my sister and I kissed Paul Stanley good night every
night from when I was 10–14 (when I left home).

KISS happened to be on the same record label that Def FX
had been on and I still had friends working there. The beautiful
Marlene, marketing director of Universal Music and my good
friend, arranged backstage passes for me and my soap-star roomie,
Krista, and we were crazy excited as we headed to the Melbourne
Sports and Entertainment Centre. In the days before smart phones
we took photos of each other with a disposable camera, sticking

out our tongues as far as we could. The concert was completely unbelievable and utterly satisfying. I was the happiest girl in the world. So was my roomie and we were both shaking with excitement as we headed backstage to meet the band. I had a copy of my bestselling book *Witch: A Personal Journey* to give to Paul. I couldn't believe that I was going to meet him in person.

Groups of people were assembled to walk into the media room and have their photo taken with the band. My girlfriend Beki from pop band The Mavis's, and their guitarist, Nic, were there too and we were all bouncing off the walls as we waited to be taken in.

When we walked in Gene pointed at me and growled, 'Is that for me?!' Argh! He scared me and I ran straight to my teen crush Paul and snuggled up against him. I still have a copy of the photo – I'm happy as a pig in mud next to Paul who has both arms protectively around me.

Paul loved my book and I left for home that night feeling like everything made sense in the world. If that little ten-year-old girl growing up in nowhereland suburban Sydney could meet her idol and give him her book, then anything was possible!

The next day Beki called me. 'FI!' she screamed. 'Gene Simmons is going to call you! He asked for your phone number last night and I gave it to him!' Before I could reply she hung up. A minute later my phone rang again. I answered, 'Hello?'

'Fiona, its Gene, Gene Simmons.'

Oh my god, even writing this all these years later my heart misses a beat! I couldn't believe it!

We chatted and he invited me to go to Brisbane with the band for their next show. The plane was leaving that night. Of course I said yes!

I was mostly excited to see Paul again – and thrilled that Gene had contacted me – but I wasn't sure what to do about Gene, who had apparently slept with over 3000 women, even back then!

That night I met him at the Ansett Business Class lounge. I walked in and there he was standing by himself sans make-up and looking like a nice Jewish boy. As I reached him he put his arm around me and I said, 'Don't touch me in public.' He took his arm away and said, 'Why not? It might be good for your career.' But at the time I was starring on a TV show and also on the cover of one of the most popular magazines in the country and I said, 'Actually, I might do you more good!' This cheeky banter got us off to a great start and cemented our friendship. Gene is incredibly intelligent and doesn't drink alcohol, so he is always lucid and present. However, he is a sex addict and I had trouble keeping him off me on the plane flight!

We got to our Brisbane hotel and entered the elevator. Gene pressed several floors. I asked him why he did this and he said it was so people following him didn't know which floor he was staying on. It was a good tip. We went to our respective rooms. I had agreed to join Gene only if he booked me a separate room. I agreed to be in a room next to him, but with no adjoining door. We sat up most of the night drinking orange juice and decaf coffee (Gene doesn't consume caffeine either), and it was great. We talked about his business empire and my Witchcraft. He said I should move to Los Angeles and he would introduce me to his agent. I pretty much made my mind up that second that I would do that. It was the third seed.

At a point I got up and went to the bathroom … and fainted! I came to on the floor with a worried Gene hovering over me. I had no idea why I fainted, but I think it was just the absolute dream-like nature of what was going on. I also hadn't been able to eat much for a couple of days. I was so excited with the surreal turn my life had taken. To his credit, Gene didn't take advantage of me when I was out cold and he gave me his arm and walked me to my room like a total gentleman before kissing me goodnight on the cheek.

The next night was the KISS concert and it was so completely awesome again. I was in the front row and Gene threw an empty water bottle at me and then copied me when I folded my arms in mock protest. Paul pointed at me when he sang 'I WANT YOU!' OOOH my god! Again, all these years later, I am tearing up and laughing with thrills at the memory of this incredible time in my life!

After the show there was a big dinner at a Chinese restaurant. I was seated between Gene and Paul and I sensed they had a bet on. They were both flirting with me! Gene finally whispered in my ear, 'I know you really like Paul, I won't be hurt if you go with him.' And an hour later I found myself going up in an elevator with Paul, who had also pressed a lot of buttons. We got into his room and he had the copy of my book beside his bed. He was so sweet and took me in his arms and … mashed his face into mine with all the subtlety of a bulldozer! He then proceeded to thrust his tongue into my mouth in the most gross and unsexy way imaginable. It was supposed to be the kiss of a lifetime and it was THE WORST KISS I have ever had! Even worse than my first kiss with Gilbert McGovern when I was 13 years old and he pinned me against the sewing room door at school, slobbering all over my chin. I guess we just didn't have the chemistry I had dreamed of when I was ten years old! What a disappointment! When he finished we both just stood there. And then I said, 'Let's go back downstairs.'

Gene looked really surprised when we came back only 15 minutes later. Paul wandered off to talk to other people and Gene asked me what had happened? I just said we didn't have chemistry. Gene took my arm in his and said, 'Well then, you are mine.' And he continued to be the perfect gentleman.

The next day I flew back home. And started making plans to move to Los Angeles.

I made the move six months later in 2001. I had reached the top of one career ladder to start firmly at the bottom of another. Gene kept his promise and introduced me to his agent, who secured a meeting for me with the Vice President of Spelling Entertainment, Jonathan Levine. Spelling Entertainment produced the TV series *Charmed* – about three sisters who are Witches. I was up for a role.

My book *Witch: A Magickal Journey* had been released in the US and was doing well; it felt like I had traction – *Charmed* had even featured it in two episodes.

But six months down the track nothing had cemented.

There was no role on *Charmed*. I knew this after the fourth meeting I had with Jonathan Levine, where he spent 45 minutes talking about himself before telling me that I should visit his house in Malibu … 'the sun sets over the ocean and the dolphins are calling your name.' Ugh. With a sinking heart I got a taste of how insincere this town is. I was used to being reasonably respected and considered useful in the Australian entertainment industry, but here I was just another blonde looking for work. This was in the heady days of Heath Ledger and other Australian actors taking LA by storm. But I wasn't an actor. My selling point, Witchcraft, was a bit more unique than being an actor – but that held me back. Whilst the 'W' word guaranteed a meeting because of the novelty factor, tangible work rarely followed. The Aussie dollar bought thirty-three American cents at the time and I was burning through my savings.

Encouraging me not to give up in this flakey, insincere town, Gene said to me, 'Fiona, I take 100 meetings and only 1 of them will be worthwhile, and I'm Gene Simmons!' And so I kept on with 'meetings' and slowly but surely I edged my way onto the US mainstream entertainment radar, touting quirky, scary Witchcraft in the most friendly and marketable way. My Australian-accented, blonde subversion to the dominant paradigm of the evil Witch was enough to land me another independent book deal: *Pop Goes The Witch*. There were also regular guest appearances on national TV shows, Ryan Seacrest pronouncing me 'Fiona, The Hot Witch' on *E! News* and regularly casting spells on KTLA 5 Morning News with now CNN darling, Michaela Pereira, and handing out Hollywood Hexes at night on radio with *Entertainment Tonight* host Leeza Gibbons. I even landed the original *Survivor* winner Richard Hatch's manager. But our partnership was short-lived – like my appearance on *Australian Celebrity Survivor* two years later.

As I got busier in the public eye I tried to create some magickal balance and I sought out the friendship of two cool occultists: Jymie Darling and her wife, Vicki, who owned the legendary and oldest occult store in California, Hollywood's Panpipes Magickal Marketplace. We became fast friends. Jymie puts together Pagan Day Fest – an annual event held in bustling downtown LA, which attracts Witches and other occultists from around the country for workshops, market stalls and just to hang out together. It is now the largest tolerance festival for the Pagan Community in Los Angeles. I was always honoured to be invited to appear at it.

I also started a small Coven, the Dark Light of Lilith Coven, with two wonderful Witches. Together we created a safe, quiet, magickal space for ourselves in the midst of hectic LA. We did Coven casting, and blood-binding rituals on the rooftop of the house I lived in just off Sunset Blvd. We met every week for a while for spellcasting work and to create a Book of Shadows together. Our everyday lives got increasingly busy but we consistently practised for some time. I ended up writing a book, inspired by our experiences, so ultimately my spiritual path became work again because, at the end of the day, that's why I was in LA: to work and to survive by being the World's Favourite Witch.

Survival meant making lists. I navigate from a multitude of self-induced and exterior-induced pits of fear, via ladders of lists. As the world falls down around my ears, these lists become a way

Alecia (aka 'Pink') and I. We were good friends through my time in Hollywood. She is a sweet, wild girl and always up for anything!

to climb out of the rubble. I love drawing large squares to the left of every 'To Do' and checking them off with a satisfying tick.

I can get to the end of the day with hell still raging in my head yet take some solace in the fact that I got all my boxes checked.

This ability to discipline myself to take action in the face of paralysing fear (of failure) also serves another purpose, as it turns out – sometimes I manifest things into action.

Nicolas Cage is an example.

As every promise that had been made was systematically revealed to be empty in my first year in Los Angeles, I wrote a list of how I was going to maximise my opportunities and secure my place as America's Favourite Witch, despite all the broken promises.

Being in Hollywood I felt, in my core, I needed to associate with people who were at a level that I thought I needed to be. This particular list included meeting Nicolas Cage, who was then working on a remake of the original Hammer horror classic called *The Wicker Man* – about Witches.

Long story short, quite late one night, not long after making this list, I got a call from a girlfriend, who said: 'Oh my god, Nicolas Cage is going to call you!' She worked for Nic's production company.

I hung up and, moments later, sitting in bed, my cellphone rang and it was Nicolas Cage.

We talked for two hours – he wanted me to drive over to his house and drink Limoncello with him.

But I didn't. Maybe I should have.

I did end up having dinner with him and his business partner, Norm, a week later. It was a disaster. I committed every faux pas.

Desperately seeking his approval, I went and got my make-up professionally done in the MAC store on Robertson. I got my hair professionally blow-dried at the Dry Bar on Sunset. I wore a dramatic, dark-red woolen dress. I tried too hard.

I turned up at the Chinese restaurant in Beverly Hills and smiled and shook hands. Then sat next to Nic and proceeded to talk about myself non-stop until it was time for desert. At which point Nic turned to Norm and said, 'Would you like to leave?' No dessert and only a brief handshake from Nic on departure.

I'd blown it. I'd let all my insecurities and my fear mask what I really needed to be – just present in the moment, relaxed and confident.

Nic had read my book and was interested in meeting me. We'd already spent two hours talking on the phone that first night, to the point of discussing how we both wanted our bodies to be eaten by sharks after we died. I didn't have to come at him like I was desperately seeking attention and approval.

He probably thought I was a bragging idiot, but I was just an insecure girl hoping that my knight in shining armour might rescue me from a slippery slope.

My biggest mistake was mentioning meeting Lisa Marie Presley at my girlfriend Pink's house and forgetting that she, for a time, had been his wife.

Anyway. I did meet Nic, so I could cross that off my list.

It just wasn't what I was hoping it would be.

I was going to have to rescue myself.

Hollywood did get more mythic: Couch-chatting with all three Charlie's Angels (Lucy, Cameron and Drew); pool parties with Pink; so many brushes with fame, and tarot-card readings with celebrities, too. Just like during that doomed dinner with Nic, I increasingly hoped that some of their lustre would rub off on me as I struggled to stay afloat in that cutthroat town. Gene and I kept in touch – I would visit his house or join him for business dinner meetings. But over time he got really busy with a new TV show (*Family Jewels*), which he wanted me to appear on but the producers thought having a Witch on the show might turn away the family audience. For all its craziness, America was very conservative when it came to potentially offending the Christian right.

However, I did end up starring in a reality TV show for the cable channel Syfy. It was called *Mad Mad House* and I was invited to be a part of it, as The Witch.

Twelve years later this TV show has a cult following and is streaming on Hulu. In 2016 a television journalist reviewed the show:

TURNS OUT THE WEIRDEST REALITY SHOW
EVER WAS ACTUALLY MADE IN 2004

*Every day on the internet feels like its own small-scale competition
to be <u>the most woke</u>. You're either on the right side of history,
or the wrong one, with no gray area in between. If you refuse
to accept the existence of gender-neutral bathrooms, same-sex
marriage, or Gaia, you are a dinosaur, a relic from America's old
guard whose time will soon, mercifully, run out. This is the new
normal, and it's not necessarily a bad thing. Get woke or get bent.*

*Now imagine a reality show on which a group of
contestants from all walks of life compete to become the most
'woke.' In which five judges who practice alternative lifestyles
determine contestants' ability to abandon their deep-seated
belief systems and not only acknowledge, but accept, the
ideas of those who exist on society's margins. The contestants'
reward is not merely a substantial cash prize, but the security
of knowing they have transcended the close-mindedness of
their stifling upbringings.*

*You'd probably find such an idea green-lightable in the
context of modern American culture, yet the show I described
above was not on NBC's Fall 2016 lineup but already exists –
and, in fact, predated the inclusively indignant internet culture
I just outlined by nearly a decade. You've never heard of it
because it wasn't marketed the way I pitched it. While such a
teaser would go over like gangbusters now, in the days before
think pieces and trigger warnings it was still OK to refer to
people who were different from us as 'freaks' without facing a
social-media boycott.*

The show in question was called Mad Mad House; its one and only season aired on the Sci-Fi Channel (now known as Syfy) in 2004.

Mad Mad House's existence as a cultural artifact reminds us of how much things have changed in 12 years – that's less than a generation. Who among us now doesn't know a witch? Or someone who, like the Modern Primitive, has riddled their body with tattoos and plugs? The Alts, then seen as freaks, now walk among the normals. Soon there will be Capital One ads directly targeted at the naturalist demographic (although there's nothing in their wallets, as they don't wear clothes or carry wallets, but that's what rebranding is for).

Megan Koester, Senior Correspondent, Hulu

Being a part of *Mad Mad House* was a remarkable experience. I was simply allowed to be a Witch. I got to explore my craft without having to fit it into other people's ideas of what it should be. I had a beautiful Witch's altar in my bedroom. I went for long walks with my snake. I had profound spiritual experiences with the other Alts and our contestants.

Well, that was the first week.

The second week the producers came to me and said, 'Everyone is getting along too well. Fiona, we need you to stir up some trouble or it won't be entertaining TV.' So, being a professional, I intentionally stirred up a little bit of confusion to make the reality more drama-ridden (for the producers' tastes).

I invoked the Dark Goddess and withdrew my favour from one of the contestants, who was pretty sure they were going to get my vote to stay every time.

I basically just stopped hanging out with them as much and

not always smiling when I saw them. That gave the story editors enough handle on the spoon to stir the pot.

However, I still loved the house so much for the freedom it gave me to be spiritual.

I had a profound experience during one of my meditation walks the second week I was in the house. I had my snake, Oscar, curled around my wrist and was sitting on a bench at the far end of the property looking out over Los Angeles. The house was on a hilltop in Los Feliz – the highest point in the LA basin and an ancient American Indian burial site. The ancestors could see the sea from this inland vantage point.

I was breathing deeply and in a meditative, calm state as I mused over what had been happening in the house. There was a lot of squabbling going on. The guests' opinions on world religions had been stirred into debate (which was what the producers wanted) and questions of right and wrong, true and false, had been raised.

Suddenly a hawk flew into my vision and landed in front of me on the stone wall – barely two feet away.

And then it spoke to me.

'Fiona, look at all the trees in the Garden.' The hawk had a masculine voice. It sounded like the Christian Father God (as I had imagined in my childhood).

I turned my head to look at all the trees – a swathe of green, brown and grey tones surrounding me.

'Do you see that the trees are different and yet all the same? An oak tree, a jacaranda tree – all different yet all united.'

I nodded.

The hawk continued.

'A tree's survival depends on its diversity. If every tree was exactly the same it would die.' I nodded again that I understood.

'So it is with my love,' said the hawk. 'My survival depends on the diversity of my love.

Every spiritual path is an instrument, and when these instruments are played together they become a symphony – a symphony of the soul – and that is my voice. The voice of God.'

A wave of comprehension washed over me. God's voice depended on diversity of expression.

The hawk tilted its head and said to me, 'Go back and share this with the others.'

I did as I was told and shared what the hawk had said, at the long dinner table where we ate our meals. It definitely affected everyone – in a positive way. And it was not included in the final edit of the show that went to air.

Ultimately, it was more important that we experienced a profound sense of unity, tolerance and respect for each other in the house, and that we took that lesson home with us when we returned to the 'regular world'.

And I have the opportunity to write about it now and share with you, dear reader!

Mad Mad House was a world within a world and when my microphone was unclipped from me for the last time I felt naked and bare. It's incredible how we all just jumped full-tilt into living and being the Alts – filmed by TV cameras 24/7.

And now here I was stepping away and attempting to find balance back in the everyday world.

As a professional working in the industry, my agent and manager made sure I milked the little boost my profile got. As a part of the *Mad Mad House* publicity jaunt I did a feature spread in US *Playboy* (as a guest celebrity I was always quick to tell people). This shoot promoted me as a Witch and there was an earthy, natural component to the shoot, which I loved. But it was not the feminist piece de resistance that the Aussie shoot had been nearly seven years before. Still, it felt good to be modeling for *Playboy* at the age of 39 – an age when women in the industry are told that we are starting to lose our commercial appeal.

Also off the back of *Mad Mad House* I got another major book deal: *Bewitch A Man*. Despite all the public marketing of my Witchcraft, and the compromises in credibility during this time, I had some of the most intensely magickal experiences of my life – including a lucid encounter with my deceased biological father, at a Salem Coven Gathering during Samhain, on Gallows Hill …

I think I was in Salem to do a book signing – I can't remember exactly how I ended up on a hill with Laurie Cabot's Coven celebrating Samhain. In my early Witchling days I had read Laurie's celebrated and respected tome *Power of the Witch* written in 1989, and I had to pinch myself that I was there meeting her. She had just had knee surgery and was seated like a queen, with Celtic blue spirals tattooed on her cheeks, confirming her absolute commitment (inside and out) to the way of her Goddess.

We cast Circle on land where the Coven had been burying crystals for years. The ground hummed with energy. But we were not where the tourists gather on Gallows Hill. We were at a place a mile away – the true Gallows Hill, where the Witches were hung, cementing Salem's place in history and folklore as America's birthplace of Witches.

A sickle moon hung yellow and low in the sky. The air was

cold but clean and pure. There were thirteen of us and one of the Coven members ran around the perimeter of the Circle brandishing a sword, carving our sacred space into being as Laurie invoked the elements.

I felt a strong hand on my shoulder, pressure that was calm and reassuring – just very strong. I thought that the sword bearer must have stopped behind me and wanted me to do something. Every Coven has different methods of Circle casting and, as I was a visitor, I was just fitting in and following everyone's lead. I turned to acknowledge the sword bearer – but there was nobody there.

The pressure on my shoulder lessened but I could still feel it as I turned my face towards the centre of the Circle.

The face of my biological father leapt into my mind and my head started to hurt. My father had passed and I had only met him twice. But he made a big impression on me, not least in my genes.

In this Samhain Circle, honouring the dead, I felt he came to me. His presence felt reassuring and encouraging – I felt a part of him.

George was known to be giving and generous – in his time and energy. In a magazine interview with Judit Korner, his wife and the mother of my three half-sisters, Judit described her beloved husband as *'a pasha with a harem of women around him. With his salons, colleges, a wife and three daughters, he was constantly surrounded by women. When the girls were at school swimming training, George would go to them with robes, hair dryers and a thermos of hot cocoa. He really knew how to anticipate your needs, and I think this is the secret behind the success of Madame Korner.'*

As I write this for the first time I think to myself, how would I feel if I had a father who had doted on me in this way? My adoptive father did not pamper or celebrate my existence. He mostly just tolerated it, sometimes despised it, and then tried to suppress it. How would I feel if I had been one of those girls – my father walking towards me with a robe, hair dryer and hot cocoa? Would I have been more careful who I gave my heart to? Would I have expected more than abuse and chased a rejecting man's approval? Would I have had a better sense of self-worth?

It doesn't contribute to my happiness or peace of mind to ponder these things. It makes me cry. I will use the power of reprogramming my thoughts and choose to be grateful for the opportunity to learn and consider that I don't deserve abuse. I have broken that cycle.

So, in that moment on Gallows Hill, I felt safe with my biological father's ghostly hand on my shoulder, surrounded by Witches in black robes under a sickle moon.

chapter six

HOLLYWOOD'S HOTTEST COUGAR

'Kiss the glitter off my lids
Spread your smile across my lips
Close my eyes and make a wish
This time it is for keeps.'

Tyra Banks was a princess to Oprah's queen of daytime talk, and had asked me for a love spell on national television (I later saw in the tabloids that her troubled relationship to a lawyer had improved and they had set a date to marry).

She had poured her intention into that spell.

Or had she?

The producers invited me back for a special episode, as a guest from the season's four most popular shows. I was thrilled and looking forward to it. I was told that a limo would pick me up at 8 am from my house in the Hollywood Hills and I would have hair and make-up done at 9 am and then we would film the episode in front of a live studio audience.

At 7 am my phone rang. Tyra herself had cancelled my invitation. She decided, as a Christian, it wasn't right to invite a Witch back onto the show.

Once again, I had been pulled in just so I could be thrown away.

My insides churned every day as I desperately sought others' approval – which contradicted so much of what I was telling other people to do when I said 'carve your own path'. Inside I was a hot mess. But a relatively social and magickally convenient one.

Word was out in Los Angeles that I was a good tarot-card reader and psychic advisor and I started getting phone calls from the 'A list'. All personal referrals. High-profile people knew I could be trusted and they would refer me to other well-known people. This still happens now. Readings and counseling became a cornerstone of my work. For everyone, not just the A list. I started to get booked at Hollywood parties and corporate events, reading cards for many drunk and coking people. It was draining and difficult work – but I said yes to everything to survive.

I would accept calls and requests for magickal help any hour of the day and night. But underneath it all, every selfless thing I did for others had an ulterior motive – I was positioning, strategising and desperately grasping at survival, for the next book deal, the next television show, a way to pay off the mounting Amex bill that I incurred keeping up appearances.

I also became the girl to call when Aussies needed help to get settled into Los Angeles. I had received help myself from Aussie actor Justin Melvey when I had arrived, and I was happy now to pay it forward and help other newcomers navigate the confusing demands of creating a credit history (basically going into debt so you could rent an apartment and get a California driver's licence and a cellphone account). How to get a social security number? Which bars were the best to meet agents? The best immigration lawyer to handle your O-1 Visa requirements? All the important stuff ...

I made some amazing friends this way. It was exciting to see them rock up in town relatively unknown and a year or two later be at the top of their game, succeeding in the most difficult town in the world. One of the sweetest and most talented people I saw make it was Andy Whitfield, who rose to starry heights as star of the hit television series *Spartacus*. It was incredible seeing the ball drop over a giant image of his face in Times Square on New Year's Eve, the year his show launched. As his star shone ever brighter he remained the most grounded and kind friend, sometimes crashing on the couch when we hung out at my place. I miss him a lot. He passed suddenly of cancer a short time after his star burned brightest, as an actor, husband and father. His wife, Vashti, spearheaded a heartbreaking and moving documentary of his short but potent life – *Be Here Now*. I cry my eyes out when I watch it. And I highly recommend seeing it, to be reminded of how precious life is and to savour every moment that you can.

As I helped other people settle in, lay roots and then shoot up taller than me in LALA Land, I also realised that as often as I felt lost and drained by this town I had also come a long way. I was, in fact, surviving. And it felt good to be helping others.

Still, I personally was feeling burned out by how superficial and shallow LA continued to reveal itself to be. I attended a trendy rooftop party just off Sunset Blvd one night. Upon walking in, a guy immediately came over to me, nursing a drink. He sized me up and down and spouted the ubiquitous LA question, 'Hey, great party – what do you do?' I took a sip of my drink and said, 'I work in a bagel store.' He looked surprised and, looking me up and down again, said, 'Uh, well you have great arms, do you work out?' And I said, 'No, it's from stacking trays of bagels. I stack over 500 of them before 8 am every day.' His eyes glazed over a little and he did the familiar 'look past' (basically sipped his drink, and looked behind me to see if there was anyone more special and more famous he should be talking to. He wandered off. Thing is, if he had turned around and seen what I was looking at behind him, up on the

Boulevard, he would have seen a giant billboard of my big head – I was starring in a TV show at the time and the party was for me.

By 2006 I was the author of five popular books on Witchcraft, had been invited to speak at Harvard University about Witchcraft in Popular Culture, and was a regular on US television screens. Yet I continued to say yes to everything that I could glean a little more fame and notioriety from, and I was excited when my Australian manager, Jason Williamson, called to inform me that I was invited to appear on Australia's *Celebrity Survivor*, in the midst of my Hollywood stint. It didn't matter that we were a motley crew that the industry would call 'C grade celebrities'. I loved filming on location in Vanuatu and living off the land. When I am asked what it was like to be on *Survivor* I can honestly say they gave us no props other than a machete, metal saucepan and bottled water (when it was decided that the stream we were to collect water from was not safe to drink). I felt so free and happy on the beach under the stars, lying on a giant banana-tree leaf (there were no towels). I even wrote a song about it:

> *the stars, so bright – ripe like cherries,*
> *I pluck them from the sky*
> *and let their sweet light blind my urban eyes*

These lyrics were for my solo album *Witchweb*, released a year later – its lyrics and melodies are my favourite of anything I've written. I was broken-hearted when I was voted off *Survivor* in the third episode; double-crossed by a fellow female castmate who I thought was a friend. I had even spent a whole afternoon trawling through the sand on our beach, with a coconut shell, looking for her waterproof mascara that she'd dropped. It was the essential 'luxury item' she had chosen to bring. I had chosen (with some nudging from the producers) my tarot cards, on the proviso I could bring them in a waterproof bag. They wanted me to have something Witchy that could be fed into the storyline. Maybe I could throw the cards and predict who would win.

I ended up burning them on the second night. A terrible storm blew in and we could not light our fire to keep warm. Everything was wet except my cards. I decided that my tribe's survival was more important than a pack of cards I'd had for twenty years.

I lit four of them and got the fire going and we survived the night. I later heard the men's team were evacuated with hypothermia.

And then I got voted off. The tarot-card burning scene was cut from the final edit.

I still have that same deck with me now – 30 years since they were gifted to me – much worn. I read them with the cards missing. I've found it actually helps my accuracy. For my sacrifice, God gave me more inner sight.

But for the TV show I hadn't learned the key to survival: that this was a strategic, political exercise, not an honest pursuit of finding food and not getting injured in a somewhat harsh tropical environment.

Five years ago when I moved to the Caribbean I found an original deck of my tarot cards online. They are not made for store stock anymore. I bought them and use them today. My original deck can't handle the wet muggy environment here – I keep them sealed in a dry container. But I keep one of the old cards in my new deck, to be a connecting thread.

Above is a picture of my thirty-year-old High Priestess card (on the left), shuffled and read thousands of times, and the five-year-old replacement, now read hundreds of times and used for readings in the humid islands. These two cards kind of sum up my magickal self – what I thought I knew is on the right, and what I know now is on the left!

Back to life as a public Witch …

As much as I increasingly received approval and acceptance as a Witch in the 'muggle' public eye – the Witchcraft community was hell bent on burning me at the stake (who needs Christians?) – attacks on my credibility and authenticity were rife. There was even a website called Fiona Horne is a Shithead.com. This wasn't news – throughout my early years I had been judged, attacked and marginalised – whether it was being nicknamed Fish Lips or the comments from Australian newspaper reporters: 'It's unlikely Fiona Horne was aware she was making a powerful political statement when she removed her top during Def FX's Big Day Out performance', and now, 'Fiona Horne is a fake – she just became a Witch to be famous', as multiple Pagan web nerds noted in their blogs critiquing my existence.

Maybe that last comment was closest to the truth, with one exception: I was already famous when I came out of the broom closet as a Witch. And while it ultimately became my meal ticket and my job, my early experiences of the Craft were pure and soul-saving: my timid searches around the alternative book stores when Def FX toured Byron Bay; my pilgrimages to legendary stores such as Panpipes in Hollywood and Eye of the Cat, in Long Beach, during Def FX's US tours; my song lyrics in 'Spiral Dance' on Def FX's first EP. But I was still guilty of magickal treason.

Back to my *Bewitch a Man* book. In the ultimate act of Witchy inauthenticity, I wrote this book while I was in a lesbian relationship. I fell in love with my female spin instructor, Stacy, convincing myself for a year that I was gay. I even did that US *Playboy* shoot when I was in a relationship with her – she was lying on the bed inside while I was out in the garden talking to the journalist about what kind of men turned me on (it was a short interview).

But the theory in *Bewitch A Man* was correct and, as it turns out, effective. Probably in the writing of the thing and the endless recounting of the 'number one love spell: "How to Manifest Your Perfect Man"' at a billion book events, my perfect man appeared! But, as usual with spellcasting and magick, there was a catch to be revealed.

What happened to the lesbian love of my life, Stacy? She took a summer job teaching spin in the Hamptons, and promptly

hooked up with a very wealthy mum with three kids. The woman left her husband for Stacy. But she and the woman are still together, I'm quite sure, so I'm glad they've found happiness. She was an interesting character in my life. From my relationship with her I learned that love is not gender specific. I'm grateful I fell head over heels for her – it was such a uniquely heady and romantic experience.

In this period of my life a deep lesson was being hammered into my lower consciousness: If you make decisions based on surviving financially and not on being authentic and honest with yourself and others, then you are carving a destructive path that will ultimately leave you unfulfilled and very unhappy, no matter how interesting and glamorous (and spiritual) your life may appear to others.

'You don't get older, you get better' was one of my favourite sayings. I was about to hit 40 and had been bouncing around weekend stands in Hollywood for six years – except for Stacy. When Stacy left me I hung out at lesbian bars and went on dates for a few months, but nothing felt sincere. LA women were just as flakey and unreliable as LA men. Months later I was desperately lonely. I was not doing any useful work on myself – just peddling my Witchy wares on an increasingly desperate scale. I was living in Jerry Seinfeld's mansion (now owned by a banker, who asked me to be a live-in manager). The banker's primary family home was in San Francisco and he had bought this house to fulfil his dream of being a 'Hollywood Producer'. I was lucky to stay on.

But I also felt like a bird in a gilded cage up there on the hill. Alone in this 7-million-dollar white palace, developing OCD and keeping the house ready for his imminent arrival and stay, which, as it turned out in the four years I lived there, was a total of nine months. When he did arrive he would say, 'Thank you for making this big place feel like home.' It was a nice compliment that I was doing my job well. But it wasn't my home. It was his. So I felt lonely and isolated most of the time.

Tara, a girl I had briefly dated after Stacy left me, called me at noon one day and suggested we drive for two hours up to Taft – a small, crystal-meth-ridden town in central California – and skydive that afternoon. I said yes immediately. When have I not been up for an adventure? For a moment, sitting alone in the multi-million-dollar Hollywood mansion that I did not own, it crossed my mind I could die – and then I remember thinking, that would be good – I'm done with this lonely, fake failure of a life. Tara and I raced north in her little red VW Beetle and, at 4 pm, I found myself strapped tightly to the chest of a rather gorgeous, very young man named Scotty, and plunging out of an aeroplane at 10 500 feet.

I loved every crazy, breathtaking, soaring moment of it.

And from then on I would make the pilgrimage to Taft every Friday afternoon for a weekend of throwing myself out of aeroplanes. Sleeping in the drop zone's bed-bug-ridden bunkhouse and sharing the communal shower block with all sorts of nefarious skydiving characters, I worked my way through my AFF A-level skydiving licence. Then I achieved my B licence, accumulating over 250 jumps in my first year. (Five years later I was to achieve a World Record in skydiving, for a challenging 13-

way head down formation in the skies of Oregon – the fact that all participants on the jump were over 40 years of age being a key part of the credit).

It was during my first months of skydiving that I would sometimes see a silver BMW pull up to the drop zone and a guy wearing a white skydiving suit with black and silver stripes running down its length would get out. I couldn't bring myself to look at him at first – he was so handsome and also the best skydiver on the drop zone. I felt so inadequate that I put my head down every time he glided past me.

But when I eventually did look into his eyes I realised I was looking at … Brad Pitt!

Not *the* Brad Pitt, but the spitting image of him.

And to cut a long story short, over the next few months we fell in love and he matched the 'man of my dreams' spell description I had written in *Bewitch A Man*, to a T.

It took a while for us to get the courage to be together. What I read as perfect aloofness in him was actually shyness – he was intimidated by me as it turns out! He told me one night when I was lying in his arms after making love, 'I would think, who is this pretty girl with the cool accent who drives up from LA and jumps by herself every weekend? She looks like she could be on TV – but people at the drop zone say she works as a spin instructor.' (I did – it was a part-time job I took while I waited, hoping for my next TV show or book deal to drop). But there was one catch: he was sixteen years younger than me. As it turned out, though, that catch was minor and he became the love of my life.

I was touted as one of Hollywood's hottest cougars in an *E!* television special, sandwiched between Demi Moore (who was dating Ashton Kutcher at the time) and Mira Sorvino (who was dating someone hot and young, but I can't remember who). As a 'talking head expert' on the show, I was given authority to judge all the other girls in the industry who were dating younger guys. But what did I know? I faked my way through that show like I often did, playing up to what I thought people expected me to be.

My first visit to Jeff's hometown of Bakersfield was in the lead-up to Halloween. On every street corner (along with a church) were posters and signs saying 'BURN THE WITCH'! The posters turned out to just be the name of a prominent high school's annual stage production, but it didn't make me feel that welcome. And I will never forget my first dinner with his conservative Baptist (he isn't) family. I was seated next to his mother, and as first course was served she turned to me and said loudly, 'So, you are 16 years older than my son – and you are a WITCH?!'

Despite this dubious welcome, I left my Hollywood career, and Jeff, and I bought a house together in Bakersfield (a convenient 40-minute drive from the drop zone). I pulled all the skills together that my adoptive mother had instilled in me and devoted myself to planting a garden, managing a home … and skydiving every weekend. I also started to fly aeroplanes. Jeff's full-time job was as a corporate pilot of business jets owned by oil and agriculture companies in the region. He was also a flight instructor and owned a Citabria Decathlon aerobatic aeroplane and we spent many happy weekends out at the desolate Shafter Airfield making the most of the uncrowded airspace, with him instructing me on loops, rolls and hammerhead manoeuvres.

My entertainment career was down the toilet but I was the happiest I could remember.

I still had all my hang-ups, fears and insecurities, but when I started to cave into them Jeff would pull me close, look me in the eyes and tell me everything was all right and he would love me forever. And I would gaze up at him and say in a little girl's voice, 'Really?' and he would look at me through his long lashes and say, 'Forever.' And I believed him.

I completely poured myself into my relationship with Jeff. I loved being a gardener (I planted magickal herbs studded between the shrubs, and made an enchanted catnip and crystal garden for the cats, which they couldn't get enough of). I wasn't doing any useful work on myself – I basically ran away from one life into another. Jeff was the answer to all my prayers and problems. And I really loved skydiving – I worked hard training towards that World Record with dedicated months of practice. I started writing for skydiving publication USPA's *Parachutist* – feature articles and cover stories – and made a lot of friends in the industry. As a couple we travelled to different drop zones and events around the country. We traveled to Belize together numerous times for the famous skydiving 'Boogie in Belize', where I jumped into the Blue Hole from 13 000 feet, meeting Jeff on a boat when I landed in the water, and donning SCUBA gear together to dive the Blue Hole, with its dramatic stalactites and big sharks.

We also did a special skydive together – enjoying a Sky Kiss at 180 miles per hour, which became a really popular photo amongst the skydiving community that year.

Jeff even came to Australia with me, where the newspapers and magazines had a field day with my 'toy boy' at that year's

Top: Jeff and I enjoying a skykiss at 180 mph; Middle: My feet at 3000ft over the Blue Hole, Belize; Bottom: My World Record – POPS Head Down 2012, I'm pointed out!

Melbourne Cup. I wore a Witch's hat instead of a fascinator. He thought it was all funny. That's why I loved him. He was so grounded and wasn't intimidated by my crazy previous life. He embraced my desire to settle down and be a regular person. It was a really amazing time of learning and sharing together.

This period of my life also marked my continued rise to the top as an international psychic phone counsellor. I realised I could have a deep, empathic connection with people, no matter where they were in the world. I shuffled my 20-year-old tarot deck thousands of times as I sat at the kitchen table, talking to

clients from all over the world on Skype and making a small financial living while my boyfriend flew jets and got paid a lot. We were very happy. During this time we even got quietly married – we didn't want anything about our lives to change. I loved being home with our two cats, taking some calls, doing some gardening, taking some calls, doing Jeff's washing and planning what to make for dinner for us – and then looking forward to him coming home.

Despite the retreat to the suburbs, I got a salubrious invitation from a notorious Witch, author and entrepreneur, Christian Day, who wanted to crown me 'Queen of the Witches' at his Salem Halloween/Samhain Ball. I was excited and flattered, and accepted.

He flew me to Salem and crowned me at a gothic extravaganza of an event that was one of the most fun and bewitching weekends I have ever had. Christian gave me the best and most magickal introduction you could wish for to a town like Salem. I took part in tea-party seances, ghost-walking tours and just fell in love with the town and Christian's world of enchanting friends. From that experience grew a strong friendship that kept me plugged into the magickal world while still willingly embracing being a housewife in suburban Bakersfield. Even as I hid away, the original Cat Woman artist and comic producer, Jim Balent, and his wife, Holly, immortalised me in their comic book series *Tarot: Witch of the Black Rose*, and dedicated a whole storyline to me. They had been at the Witches' Ball and seen me crowned.

They are such a cool couple – I was honoured and it was also a lot of fun. They sent me the script for the comic and Jeff took photos of me acting out the various 'positions' that Jim needed to draw his pictures of me, that Holly would then colour. There were

over 500 photos in the end. I never knew so much work went into making a comic strip!

In 2010 the economy collapsed and Jeff's job changed. He was away on corporate flights all the time – we hardly saw each other – and I started to feel very lonely and insecure.

I began making the two-and-a-half hour drive down to Los Angeles every week to try to drum up some business. I still had an agent and I was trying to sell TV rights to my books. *Bewitch a Man* was optioned by The CW network to be developed into a sitcom, but it didn't get past development stage. As is the way in Hollywood, another writer came out with a copycat project called *Spellbound* and it nixed mine. On top of that career slight I also experienced a major double-cross by a real-estate agent who I brought a buyer for the Seinfeld mansion to. He promised me a gift on the multi-million-dollar sale and, as my income had dwindled dramatically, I was relying on him being good to his word. He wasn't – and then told me I was breaking the law asking for money. I had no idea that what he had suggested was not legal. I hung my head, accepting yet another victim scenario, and walked away.

I started to drink more and more. The best way to forget my woes was to pour a big Magic Mimosa (a large glass of champagne with a splash of orange for colour) and do some gardening. If Jeff wasn't flying he would join me – we both were drinking more when we saw each other. We kept up appearances if we were heading out to a local wine bar with his friends, but I would sit silently feeling like a square peg in a round hole as they all waffled on about nothing I could relate to. I felt lost and he was no longer enough to make me feel unquestionably secure. I started to regret walking away from my life before Jeff, but I was deeply confused because I wasn't sure if my life before him was that good anyway. I often succumbed to dark fits of depression coupled with uncontrollable crying. Most of them he didn't see – but he saw enough. When he would find me sobbing in the wardrobe he would stand there helplessly. But as disjointed as things felt, I still loved him very much. But he was falling out of love with me, as I was to find out in an excruciatingly painful way.

My parents came to visit, all the way from Australia, in September of 2011. I was so excited to be welcoming them to our home. It was the first time they had ever come to visit me in all the years I had lived in the USA. Mum and I had plans to work on the garden together. When she arrived we headed straight out to Lowes to buy bulbs and trays of seedlings. Jeff was away on a work trip for the first part of their visit, but when he got back we all headed up to Yosemite National Park to stay at a beautiful little bed and breakfast on the river. We would spend a night together as a family and then Jeff would head back down to Fresno to fly to Chicago – his next contracted flight.

It was a lovely evening. Mum and Dad were about to celebrate their fiftieth wedding anniversary and I felt so happy sitting with my handsome partner and my ebullient parents who, despite our fractured and difficult relationship in my younger years, felt like dear, beloved friends to me, in this moment. I was careful to not rub my dad up the wrong way and he was relaxed and the trip was unfolding beautifully. Some of Mum and Dad's marital success rubbed off on my guy and me; we made love that night for the first time in a while, and fell asleep in each other's arms. As I drifted off to sleep I could hear the river and life was beautiful and perfect.

Jeff had to be up at 5 am to drive to the airport and I awoke as he kissed me goodbye on the forehead. As the front door closed behind him I got up and went to the bathroom. He had showered and in the steam on the mirror he had traced the words 'I love you.' Like I had every day since I had met him, I contemplated how blessed I was to know him and to love him – for better for worse, through good times and bad. It was worth the seven years of loneliness before Jeff, to be so loved now. It was good that I had given up 'me' for 'us'.

I joined Mum and Dad for breakfast on the patio and then we made our way into the park for a scenic tour we had booked. I had never visited Yosemite and it was stunningly beautiful – the soaring peaks, the verdant green valleys, the animals – all of nature, harmonious and joyous. In the face of El Capitan – a large granite monolith – I saw a heart and snapped a photo of it to send to my guy.

We ate lunch at a fabulous lodge on the outdoor deck facing an open field. Deer were grazing nearby and birdsong filled the air. Suddenly a large bird caught my eye. It was flying towards us along the stream and, as it got closer, I realised it was a duck – a beautiful big green duck. I had a moment to think how strange it was to see a duck flying alone like this. My eyes followed it as it flew full force into the wall of the building above my head and fell at my feet, its neck twisted and broken.

I couldn't breathe.

A lady was there and screamed out, 'Call a ranger!'

I dropped to my knees in front of the bird. The lady was now cradling its head in her hands. She was crying. 'He's dying.'

We were both crying. And then a shudder passed through the beautiful bird and it died.

And in that instant I knew something was horribly wrong – this was a terrible omen. Nothing in my life would ever be the same again.

And I was right – Jeff disappeared.

The guy who called me every night when he was on the road was nowhere to be found. I didn't worry until mid-morning the day after he had left. I called his cell and it went straight to voicemail. I checked FlightAware, an online aviation scheduling service, and it noted that his plane had arrived safely in Chicago. At least I knew he wasn't dead in a crash. Another day passed and I was frantic with worry. I called his mother, Peggy, who had become a close friend, and asked if she'd heard from him and she hadn't. I called his boss and he said that as far as he knew everything was fine and on schedule – Jeff would be flying back to Bakersfield the next day. Then, after another couple of agonising hours, Jeff called. He told me he had lost his phone. But something didn't sit right.

chapter seven

THE BROKEN-HEART SYNDROME

'You dont love me the way that I love you
I'm scared to look into your eyes
in case what I think is really true.'

'We have more problems than a dinner together can fix.'

'What do you mean?'

'We just do.'

'Darling, please don't give up on us.'

That phone call between me and Jeff marked the start of a most heartbreakingly brutal end to our relationship. After a lot of denial and sporadic periods of 'togetherness' I was to find out that he was having an affair with the daughter of his boss, who was a very young and very rich girl. She had grown up on the private plane Jeff was in charge of flying.

No amount of psychic readings or Witchcraft can prepare you or guide you through the shock and grief of complete rejection and the destruction of a life together.

If anything, psychic readings became detrimental, and the Witchcraft a distraction from what was really needed: a complete psychic shift (in me). Because, as the love of my life ended, every single character defect and flaw was revealed in me. Everything I had been able to white-lie my way through was exposed – every self-destructive, victimised, people-pleasing way of thinking. During my time with Jeff I was functioning on the premise that I needed to be in a relationship to be complete. That if a significant 'other' wasn't loving me, I was a failure.

Jeff had come into my life after seven years of me being single (with men). I really thought he was the answer to all my problems. What a horrible burden I placed on him. I handed him my huge bleeding heart and said, 'Don't drop it, don't hurt it and don't break it.' With pressure like that of course it would slip out of his hands.

The year Jeff stopped loving me, 2011, also saw the swift death of my dear friend Andy Whitfield. I didn't think my heart could be broken more when I stood up on stage at a large charity event to be 'auctioned off' as crew for a charity scenic jet flight which Jeff would captain, with me as 'flight attendant'. The jet had been donated by the owner, a good friend. Of course Jeff wasn't at the event. I had to go to it myself. My sweet girlfriend Donna took Jeff's ticket and came as emotional support for me. A giant picture of Jeff standing in front of the jet was projected onto the wall behind me as a spotlight shone on my face and we got auctioned off for $64,000 for the Children's Hospital of Orange County. I sat back down on my seat and my Blackberry lit up with a note from a friend saying, 'Hey, I just saw your friend Andy has died.'

I don't know how I managed to get up from that table but I found a quiet corner next to an elevator and sat on the floor in my fancy evening dress and just cried and cried.

Life felt unjust and cruel.

And then I developed a lump in my chest, which was suspected as cancer. Mammograms, a biopsy – all inconclusive. Mystery that it was, the doctor decided it needed to get cut out. I got very sick and was in terrible pain. I was scheduled for surgery but ended up being rushed into hospital ahead of the date. The lump turned out to be a blood clot. Discussing the results with me a day after the operation, the surgeon said, 'When we opened you up you looked like you had been in a car accident.' I said, 'I haven't been, but my husband has left me – maybe it's my broken heart.' I remember him raising his eyebrows and mentioning research on a phenomenon called 'the Broken-Heart Syndrome'. He directed me to an online article about it that had been published in the *New York Times*.

I was released from hospital on Christmas Eve. The fourth anniversary of when Jeff and I had moved into our home together. I was helped inside by Jeff's mother. I had tubes in my chest and bags of blood draining on each side. Our cats, Manny and Charlie, ran to me, weaving around my legs. But Jeff was not there. He had not called me before or since my operation. His mother did not know where he was.

He came over the next day, Christmas Day, and said he had moved out. I was lying on the couch in a deadened, shocked state, and heavily medicated. I just looked at him. He stayed only a few minutes and then asked me if I needed anything. I remember murmuring, 'A glass of water.' He brought me one and then he was gone.

The man who had convinced me he was the most loving, caring, sweet, kind person in the world, was a cruel, cold-hearted monster. But that didn't stop me from loving him and trying to win him back.

I couldn't eat – everything tasted like rubber. For two months I couldn't drive or lift anything and had to regularly visit the specialist to make sure the condition wasn't recurring. I lost a ton of weight. My girlfriends called it 'The Grief Diet'. Finally I was allowed to drive. I weighed 105 pounds, down from my usual 125 pounds. I had started to drink a lot. I would drive the five minutes to Trader Joes and buy three $15 bottles of wine, which soon became five $10 bottles, which soon became ten $3 bottles. Six months after Jeff left, I had become a full-blown alcoholic, blacking out and coming to – covered in bruises.

Incredibly, I was still working as a phone psychic, and quite busy. Other people's problems would eclipse mine. I found myself giving them the advice I should've been taking myself. In my quarter-of-a-century-old deck I saw their futures getting better, but not mine. I was firmly attached to not living in the moment. The moment was too painful and so I lived in my past and my clients' futures. Reading the cards took my mind off the grief, briefly. It was the only way I could make money to survive. I found that alcohol, for a short period, could lower the boundaries between the worlds and allow a kind of enhanced psychic connection. But over time it became a distraction, not an asset, in connecting with others. I would read for people during the day, but by nighttime I was too drunk and would pass out.

My girlfriends were amazing during this time.

My closest and most patient girlfriend, Sarah (who authored a funny and poignant book titled *Psychic Junkie* – the irony of our close friendship was not lost on us), would read for me every now and again. We would try to piece together my life and find a way for me out of the hole.

Another girlfriend CJ had taken a job as a seaplane pilot on the island of St Croix in the Caribbean. She urged me to visit. I was given the all clear from the doctor to travel, and a new prescription for a truckload of Xanax and Ambien. I spent ten days on this beautiful island, most of which I don't remember. I do remember meeting a guy and running around the island with him in a drunken haze for most of the time. I remember telling him I was a Witch and that he had looked worried and said, 'Don't tell anyone that, here – the locals don't sit good with that stuff. They do voodoo here.' But that was about as magickal as my trip was – except that this island, St Croix, left an imprint on me. It is a funny place – not touristy like the surrounding islands such as the cruise-ship-laden St Thomas, the celebrity-ridden St Barth and Richard Branson's hide-out, the BVIs. There was an oil refinery on St Croix, but that was closing. Its inhabitants were mostly locals and a raggedy bunch of ex-pats, who mostly came from Michigan and North Carolina. It was a long way from Bakersfield but it was also kind of working-class conservative. It seemed a bit lost. Like me. The locals would say 'we're all here because we're not all there'. I decided I liked it a lot.

My girlfriend Beki – from The Mavis's (who by now had also moved to Los Angeles in pursuit of bigger dreams in the entertainment industry) told me about a counselor based in Santa Monica, who could help me get Jeff back. And another girlfriend, Shelleylyn Brandler, paid for me to have 10 sessions (I was completely broke). I used to call my counselor, Brandon, like my clients called me. I don't know if he had legitimate credentials, but it helped to talk to a man who appeared relatively objective. He helped me understand that I couldn't make Jeff change – I could only change myself and work towards attracting Jeff back that way.

I was so blessed to have these patient, good friends – maybe it was my magickal karma for lending my shoulder to thousands of clients hurting in love. Because really that's what 99.9% of the calls were about: Love and the loss of it; love and the desire for it. No one called if their love life was going well.

In the middle of this dark year something else incredible happened. I became a rock star again.

Def FX did a fifteen-year reunion tour. As bleak and dark as life was, this was happening. I had agreed to it before Jeff left me. An Aussie promoter had put it together; the other three members (including the original bass player, Marty, and two new recruits) had rehearsed in Australia. I got there a week before the tour started, and thank god we had great chemistry. The second we started playing our hit 'Surfers of The Mind' in the warehouse building in St Leonards, where we were rehearsing, we knew it was going to work. Marty had called in his good mate Wiley to be the guitarist. They had played together in other bands and had their musical chemistry locked in. We were lucky to have electronic music guru Ant Banister on board, replacing the co-founder on programming, keyboards and vocals. I remember back in 1990, Ant had his electronic music collective, Clan Analogue, playing at venues, and our co-founder was always referring to him and appropriating his methods and style. By having Ant in Def FX we had something even better – we had the true original Australian electronic music force.

As Def FX we did three rehearsals and off we went around the country.I drank my way through it, but it also provided a good distraction from my grief. The crowds were huge, the music rocked, the boys and I were having a great time, laughing and loving being on the road. The enthusiasm was incredible from

Top: So amazing to perform with my brothers in rock again! Marty, Ant and Me.
Middle: It's all the yoga! Bottom: Def FX fans are the best
All photos: Rob Wilmshurst and Dean Perkins

original designer of some of my most outrageous costumes, my beloved Mindy McTaggart, gave me some new amazing creations to wear on stage. Again my ability to white-lie my way through life and pretend to be something I wasn't, stepped up. It was so surreal. Def FX had ended so badly – I never thought in a million years that we would get the chance to do this again. I was so grateful and so terrified. I look back at photos from this tour and I look like my cartoon character on stage. It's like I had to pull every mask out of the bag to do this.

Getting back to Bakersfield from Australia, all the grief and shock flooded back in and I couldn't eat again. Food tasted like cardboard. Wine like vinegar, but at least it was wet. I focused on trying to win Jeff back. Through the haze I decided I would pass the essential written exam to get my private pilot's certificate. Jeff used to tease me that I had logged 100 hours flying with him but without 'the written' it meant I wasn't serious about being a pilot. I thought if I went and passed the written that it might make him love me again. I weighed 100 pounds and had to sit on a folded towel because my bones stuck through my skin so painfully, but I studied and attended American Flyers 'pass the written' weekend school. I hadn't been in a school environment for over 25 years and I was terrified. But behind all the craziness and grief I loved aviation. And my gift at manufacturing myself to be something different to who I truly am, served me well; I interacted with the teacher and other students in the class room. I took the test the following week and I passed with the lowest possible score – 70%. But it was a pass.

It didn't make Jeff fall back in love with me. But this time was the beginning of a light shining in my life. As my biological mother had told me when I met her: 'If you can't see the light at the end of the tunnel, crawl through it and light the bloody thing yourself.' I had lit the light, but, as it turned out, the tunnel was a super black hole and I got sucked back into it, even deeper and further down, before I could start crawling out.

○

After Jeff left I tried to do things that we used to do together. When I was well enough, I started skydiving again. But there was no joy in it anymore for me. But for some reason I pushed myself to keep doing it. Missing him all the time.

One weekend I jumped out of an aeroplane with ten other girls … joining 30 girls in all, who had jumped out of two other aeroplanes 14 000 feet above Skydive Elsinore, California.

It was the All Girls Sunset Track – a feature of the annual Chicks Rock Boogie I had attended the previous three years with Jeff. I was dangerously sad and distracted, but trying to keep up appearances to my friends.

We tracked across the sky as the sun hung low – we were following a leader and making a triangle trail of speeding humans behind her.

I trailed behind a little – I wasn't keeping my body straight and flat enough – and finally as the group pulled away from me I checked my altimeter and saw I was at 7000 feet. I still had a few more thousand feet – at least another 15 seconds – before I would need to deploy my chute. But I looked around and saw I was still a few miles away from the drop zone (DZ). I decided to pull high and give myself room to fly my canopy back towards the DZ so that I wouldn't land off field in the dark. I knew when I landed the sun would be well below the surrounding coastal mountains.

And so I did a barrel roll, checking no one was tracking above me, and I looked from left to right, waved off over my head and reached back to my right hip, grasping my pilot chute handle and giving it a strong pull. Releasing the handle, I stretched my arms forward and waited for the familiar 'tug and inflate' feeling as my small pilot chute pulled my main canopy out of its case and it opened over my head.

But nothing happened.

I was still roaring toward the earth. I could feel something banging on my back and thought that maybe my pilot chute was caught in an air burble behind me. I have a pull-out system that requires me to pull the pin, releasing the small pilot chute clear of my body's wake so that it can catch air – the force of that inflating pulls my main canopy out.

So, with my belly facing the ground, I wiggled and tried to ease my pilot chute out from behind my back.

Still nothing.

I looked over my right shoulder and I saw a tangled mass of lines and a half-locked canopy bag with my main chute half hanging out.

I thought, okay I have to chop this. I checked my altimeter and I was at 3000 feet – I had 1000 more feet before I reached my hard deck of 2000 feet. I had 8 seconds before I hit the ground.

I put my right hand on my cutaway handle at my ribcage, and my left on the reserve deployment handle. And I thought for a second.

Do I want to save my life?

Jeff had left me. I was in despair without him. I was drinking night and day, even skydiving under the influence right now.

Did I want to live?

I couldn't imagine life without him.

I could die now by not cutting away and just deploy my reserve into the mess of my main canopy. It would just look as if I had an 'out of sequence' reserve cutaway event. I would be just another dead skydiver.

But then I realised that Chicks Rock Boogie would have a death associated to it and I didn't want to give the organisers that hassle … And then I thought about me … and as fucked as everything was, I decided I wasn't quite ready to die. I would find out what life was going to be like without Jeff. I decided to cut away.

I pulled hard on the right handle and released the malfunctioning mess. As soon as I felt it clear and my body pick up speed in its fall rate, I pulled the left handle and 'boom' – my orange PD Optimum reserve was over my head – inflating beautifully and with just 800 feet to go. I flew over a thousand feet of grass, coming to flare for a graceful stand-up landing at the very far end of the airport.

I looked around for my main and saw its half-inflated mess still floating in the sky half a mile away. I tried to see where it came to rest so I could drive out with someone later and find it.

As I describe this it seems to have all taken a very long time, but the events and thought processes occurred in less than 30 seconds. Time slows down on a skydive.

I gathered my reserve and started the long walk in the twilight towards the lights of the hangar. Then I saw a guy standing in front of me – a really handsome, tall guy. And at his feet was a cooler of beer. He smiled at me and I said, 'I just had my first cutaway.'

He said, 'Well then, you deserve a beer!'

I took an icy cold one that he had cracked open for me. I asked him what he was doing standing there in the dark and he said he was with the military training group and it was his job to hand the guys beers after the last jump of the day. But they had all landed off field.

I said, 'I'm glad you were here for me, then.' And he said, 'Me too.'

We ended up sleeping together that night. It was a good way to get over my ex (a little), choose life and have sex with a hot Marine!

I got sober not long after that event and I focused more on *flying* aeroplanes than jumping out of them. Whenever I take myself back to this moment, when I had a choice between living and dying, I am grateful to have chosen the former.

chapter eight

THIS WILL BE THE BEST THING THAT HAS EVER HAPPENED TO YOU

'Her life is a vast charade
She's only loved for what she fakes
But she wants to be something
She will do anything ...'

t was July 4 and I was in the kitchen with Suzy Cameron, filmmaker James 'Jim' Cameron's wife – at their ranch in Hollister. She and I were opening a bottle of Veuve Clicquot Grande Dame champagne and I was waffling on in a way that I hoped was impressing her, but I was drunk. She is a very nice lady and didn't seem to mind that I had been drinking all day and was three sheets to the wind as she poured me another glass and we kept chatting, but I cannot remember a word of what our conversation was about. I had been staying at the ranch with friends who were working for Jim as he finished up the production of his expedition to the deepest part of the ocean, the Mariana Trench. I did a few odd jobs, but essentially I was staying there to be away from the Bakersfield house and all its memories. I was drinking from morning to night and taking three Xanax tablets a day, prescribed for the debilitating panic attacks I was having. I was an animated zombie. Alone, I would cry constantly. With others I was drunk but not too inconveniently messy.

However on this night I got very messy. Here I was a guest at Jim Cameron's lovely home, and I ended up blacking out and leaving the glass Suzy had poured my champagne into, somewhere in the garden.

The next day my friends told me I had been okay and seemed to be having a good time. That I had nothing to worry about. But I have zero memory of it. There was one guy working for Jim who I was hanging out with a bit. He was also a drunk – but an angry drunk. One day, when he was in a good mood, he said I should join him and go to Baja California to stay at Jim's assistant's house. They all owned property down there after filming *Titanic*. I went, and for a few days it was fun and helped me not think about Jeff. But the drinking was out of control and now it included tequila. We drove south down the Baja peninsula to remote beaches – both wasted. He would get to a degree of drunkenness where it looked like a black cloud had sunk over his face. He was bitter and cruel and nothing I did was okay.

One night I came to, lying on a hotel bed. The light was on and I had blood down the front of me. The guy was sitting at the foot of the bed looking panicky. I tried to speak but I couldn't move my jaw. I had no idea what had happened. I managed to get up, almost falling over I was still so drunk, and went to the bathroom. I looked in the mirror and my chin was split open and swollen. I wondered had he punched me in the face?

He said, 'I was asleep and then there was a knock at the door. One of the barmen had you over his shoulder. He dumped you on the bed and ran out.'

If the guy hadn't hurt me who had? I tried to remember the night. The guy had stormed off in a self-induced huff earlier. I had stayed at the bar playing pool with some American students. I remember talking to a group of Mexican men and drinking tequila with them. Then nothing.

I was sore all over and wondered if I had been raped. I shut the bathroom door and pulled down my jeans. Everything seemed intact there. I really had no idea what had happened.

The next morning I went to the hotel manager. I explained I had been in a bad way the night before and one of his staff had brought me to my room. I asked him if he knew more about what had happened? He told me that I had been drinking with the Americans and doing tequila shots. Just as I was about to do another shot I passed out and smashed my chin on the bar as I fell to the floor. I was out cold.

I have absolutely no memory of this.

I was ashamed and apologised profusely. But he politely said, 'It is no trouble, madam.' This horrible event didn't stop me drinking for the rest of our trip. When I look back at photos I look so red and swollen – bloated with alcohol. My eyes are dead. My teeth stained red with wine.

Arriving back in California the guy went back to Australia – and we parted ways with a vague promise of getting together again. But I knew he was really bad news for me – and I wasn't bringing out the best in him. Better that we never saw each other again.

I left the Bakersfield house and stayed at a girlfriend's in the Hollywood Hills. She kindly gave me a job helping her with home-office chores for her property-listing company that did contracts for photo shoots and films. I was renting her small studio cottage with the pay she gave me. During my lunch break I would walk across the driveway and chug down a few glasses of white wine. She must have known what I was doing. She hardly drank alcohol. I must have stunk. But she was a kind friend and let me stay.

I kept drinking harder and harder. Once I was at my girlfriend's bachelorette party at a trendy Beverly Hills bar and was chatting loudly with a guy next to me, having a great time, when he turned to me and said, 'You're spilling your drink.' I followed his gaze and realised my wine glass was hanging by its stem upside down in my hand – the contents of an expensive Napa Cabernet Sauvignon had been poured into my fake Prada purse. I looked back at him and noticed that, rather than being enthralled by my company, as I had thought he was, he looked like he wanted to be anywhere else in the world rather than standing next to me.

I stumbled out of there and drove home – I don't actually remember driving. I just remember waking up on the floor next to my bed.

I was really sick.

Somewhere in the repetitious blur that followed, I got a call from an old friend who was a hugely successful music executive. He was in town for a couple of days and wanted to catch up.

In advance of our lunch date I gulped down an entire bottle of white wine while standing at the fridge, pushing my fist into my stomach to distract myself from the burning pain there.

I was careful to order only one glass of Pinot Grigio as we ate on the beautiful patio at the Sunset Marquis Hotel's restaurant. I was chatting loudly about myself, telling him how the band tour went, about my recent teen-fiction book release. Waffling on. He cut me off mid-sentence and with a penetrating look said, 'Fi – how are you really?' I stopped. I wanted to burst into tears. I took a deep breath and, looking down, I said quietly, 'I think I drink too much.'

He asked me if I would do him the great honour of meeting a good friend of his. His friend was a manager of successful music artists and someone he had found to be quite an angel in the world. There were no promises but maybe this man could help me feel better.

I rang the number and made an appointment to meet his friend the next day. Again I gulped down a bottle of wine ahead of the meeting. I wore a long black summer dress to hide my bloated stomach and legs I had developed from so much drinking and so many Xanax pills. I turned up at the chic Hollywood loft office at 3.30 pm, managing to be on time.

I wondered if my friend had set me up for a job interview – that this guy was my ticket back into the industry. But instead, this man became my first sponsor, helping me to join AA. He promised me that it would be the best thing that would ever happen to me.

Alcoholics Anonymous – the smirking joke among my Hollywood drinking friends was that AA was a cult for weak people who couldn't handle their liquor. The mysterious meeting place, called the Log Cabin, was on a side street in Hollywood and where, the cynics told me, untold celebrities went to meet a producer or director for their 'next big break'.

Maybe you have a similar opinion. Or maybe you are curious. Maybe what I share with you will help you. Or just add another layer to my story … it's just what helped me.

The man told me to go to a meeting … that night. He suggested one on the corner of Melrose and Heyworth – smack bang in the middle of trendy West Hollywood.

I did what he told me.

I was so nervous. The corner was actually a huge community centre, and as I walked inside I saw around three hundred people … all men.

I sat in the very back row and a bunch of sweet queenie guys handed lollies up and down the row for the whole meeting.

I listened. It wasn't like church – a little bit more like a very large gathering of friends.

The first man spoke and he was very handsome, intelligent, HIV positive and sober. His story was inspiring. And then the second man spoke and he was very funny and sober.

At the end of the meeting everyone stood up and held hands and said The Serenity Prayer.

God grant me the serenity to accept the things I cannot change,
The courage to change the things that I can,
And the wisdom to know the difference.

As the crowd started to disperse, the sweet queen with spiked punk hair and black leather jacket standing next to me said, 'Honey, we love having you here, but you may enjoy the women's meeting on the next corner!' I had been sent to the men-only meeting.

But it didn't matter. They made me feel welcome. The man had said, 'Make sure you get the Big Book and the 12 and 12'. Dutifully I walked to the front of the stage – there was a guy selling books. I asked for them but realised I had no money. He gave them to me anyway, insisting that it would be his gift to me. As he handed them over he said, 'Just keep coming back.' When I showed up at the Log Cabin for the 7.30 am meeting the next day, I was already a sweating mess and detoxing hard. There were no famous people (none that I recognised, anyway), just a lot of people trying not to drink – one day at a time. I did what I was told and kept coming back, with my sponsor's help, and ultimately the help of the people at the 7.30 am meetings, who, it turned out, did include some major celebrities who I had no idea were sober.

These high-profile people, like everyone else, maintained their sobriety by humbly attending meetings and helping newcomers like me. I made it through 90 meetings in 90 days. The program works if you work it. I had hit absolute bottom – AA was the only ladder out of my black hole.

As time went on and my sobriety grew from three months to six months, I knew I had found true magick. I was casting the biggest transformation spell I ever had.

AA redefined my life completely and gave me the opportunity to be the authentic, credible person I deep down wanted to be. There were no more thoughts of not being good enough and needing to white-lie my way through life to convince others I was tolerable and interesting. For the first time I allowed my crazy conflicted ego to step aside, and to ask honestly and sincerely for help. I am still so incredibly grateful to AA and to every alcoholic who has contributed to its existence. AA also awoke in me trust in the Universe – that I didn't need to doubt there was a 'God' – I didn't need to call myself an atheist Witch anymore. I could allow myself to experience a tangible spiritual presence in my world, that was loving and supportive and wanted the best for me, not the worst.

During my third week of sobriety, I spoke with my new sponsor – a female – the man had suggested I would be more comfortable working through the steps with her. I was feeling terrible that day and she patiently listened as I raved on about my self-loathing and self-disgust – and how I wouldn't drink just so I could punish myself; drinking would only alleviate my pain. She promised this feeling would pass and I told her I would stick to the program for one more day. And I went to the meeting that was closest to me. Another men's meeting. I was sweating and feeling so fucking terrible.

I just wanted to run out of the hall and my feet were tapping on the floor, urging me to get up and get out. The man in front of me then turned and, as if he could read my mind, smiled, reached over and squeezed my hand. I stayed. And then I had what AA calls a 'God Shot'. There was a voice speaking inside me, clear as day. It said, 'It's okay, Fiona. I know you are sick and can't hear me sometimes – but I want you to know I've got your back. You are in my arms. I've got you. You are not alone. You are safe and I will take care of everything.' I sat there shaking, but I trusted those words. And then a speaker took the podium and talked about loneliness and fear – and how his idea of God would not abandon him.

When I got into my car after the meeting I leaned my head against the steering wheel. I was so exhausted. And then I just started to cry. But they were tears of relief, not tears of pain.

A week after that I had what is called a 'pink cloud' experience. When I joined AA I considered myself an atheist. Being brought up Catholic I ultimately rejected the Church and patriarchal God concepts and was drawn to pre-Christian Paganism, Goddess worship and polytheism. This then morphed into an idea and strong belief that the Gods and Goddesses were human constructs, projections of our minds and social, cultural evolution. As such there was no 'other, higher, bigger' – just us. When we die we see what we think will happen in those final moments before shutdown.

Throughout this dismantling of God, I still had profound sensations of ecstatic consciousness and spirituality. I came to call myself spiritual, not religious. I thought not believing in God to be a pragmatic, sensible and responsible thing to do. And I felt alone, very alone in the Universe.

Within eleven days of joining AA and starting to explore steps one and two, I had a profound and tangible God-conscious connection.

Step One:
Admitted we were powerless over alcohol and our lives had become unmanageable.

Step Two:
Came to believe that a power greater than ourselves could restore us to sanity.

I was at idyllic Drakes Beach in Hollister and it was a beautiful, sunny day. I sat on the sand reading the Big Book and *Grapevine* (a monthly AA publication featuring stories known as 'shares', written by AA members). I was thinking about AA, God, The Steps, not drinking, my life.

I was feeling very connected to the natural beauty of the sea and I decided to try 'talking' to God.

I thought of the St Francis Prayer often said at meetings and I recited a few words from it. 'God, make me a vessel of your peace.' I waited and nothing seemed to happen. I just felt alone in a beautiful place.

I decided to try again, more spontaneous and heartfelt now.

'God, what would happen if I stopped resisting you and denying that you exist?'

And as clear as day, a voice inside my head said, 'We get to work.'

I felt immediately thrust into a parallel universe – the sunlight sparkles on the water reflected off my skin as I rose and floated down the beach. My feet glided over the sand. Not touching it. Maybe this is how Jesus felt, walking on water. I don't mean this comment to sound self-aggrandising – I actually mean it seriously. I am not kidding – I could not feel the ground under my feet, yet I was moving across it. The way I was experiencing the physical universe in that moment completely changed; there was nothing solid – only energy. It was like my experience learning Vipassana – except this was even more completely magickal, especially because it was borne out of so much suffering and illness.

I stayed in this extraordinary 'present/gift' for some time. And then thoughts of fear, regret and resentment crept into my head. I caught myself, as the voice said, 'It's okay – just breathe and stay in the moment.'

I said to the voice, 'All those times I had wise words for myself, was that me speaking or you?'

And the voice said, 'I am You.'

Once again I was doused in diamond sparkles and I felt a profound sense of something 'other', something bigger than me, that loved me and would take care of me, and I knew I would never have to feel completely alone again.

AA is a spiritual program, and each person's individual idea of God is accepted. My God is no longer someone else's vengeful, punishing, judgmental presence in my life. My understanding of God is not a gender-specific image or sound. My God is strong, wise, compassionate, patient, gentle, caring, aware and present – a presence who has my back.

My pink cloud lasted a few days … and then I was thrust back into the hell inside my head and my body screaming for me to drink.

But I had recognised and heard the voice, I knew there was a way out and I could find it again.

I would not drink.

My idea of God speaks loudly and shines brightly to me in places of natural beauty. It's the same presence I communed with when I was a little girl growing up in the Australian bush. So many times in my life I lost sight and feel of it. But now, in sobriety, I am able to experience it always beside me, or, more accurately, inside me.

My idea of God will keep growing the rest of my physical life, ever more present, as I work to be a useful channel of peace, health, love and harmony.

I have let go of all the regrets and half-truths and I just aim to be honest, authentic and accountable. Four-and-a-half years later, sobriety as I experience it now has woven all the threads of my life into something I am happy – and grateful – to wear.

I remember when I first got sober I didn't want people to know I had given up drinking altogether. I would go out with drinking friends and when they ordered their beers and wine or whatever, I would say, 'I'll have a soda. I'm taking a break from drinking today.' I was worried I would alienate people, that I would come across as weird and inconvenient if I said I was sober – that it would be an admission of failure that I could not drink 'normally' like 'everyone else'. If you have got this far in the book you have probably accepted that I'm weird. Haha! So I'm confident you won't mind that I got sober and that I stay sober by applying what I learned in AA. Alcoholics Anonymous didn't 'teach me' as much as 'unteach' me. It helped me let go of a lot of falsehoods that I had padded myself with to function in society in a half-light way.

I wrote the following at 100 days sober:

30 January 2013

Other than a headache (from training at the spin studio!) I feel very good.

Every day sober, the bar is raised on what 'feeling good' is.

Everyone I know who has done what the program suggests is happier in their hearts, minds and bodies; that happiness permeates their environment.

There will still be different personalities and different likes and dislikes. We AA-ers are not all zombies walking around trying to be the same.

We've just learned to stay ... in an environment that brings out the best in us, not the worst.

We talk about having a 'spiritual awakening'. It can be described as having the following symptoms:

1. *An increased tendency to let things happen rather than make them happen.*

2. *Frequent attacks of smiling.*
3. *Feelings of being connected, with others and nature.*
4. *Frequent, overwhelming episodes of appreciation.*
5. *A tendency to think and act spontaneously rather than from fears based on past experience.*
6. *An unmistakable ability to enjoy each moment.*
7. *A loss of ability to worry.*
8. *A loss of interest in conflict.*
9. *A loss of interest in interpreting the actions of others.*
10. *A loss of interest in judging others.*
11. *A loss of interest in judging self.*
12. *Gaining the ability to love without expecting anything in return.*

Last year it was an amazing (and sobering) experience to go through personal band- and Witchy memorabilia that had been packed away for over a decade. Normally I would look at it all with a sinking heart, thinking that I looked and sounded like a fool, or feel frustrated that I only had the double-page spread and not the cover of the magazine … and then go off and pour a giant glass of wine so I could drown my sorrows. But now I was able to look at all this stuff with a cup of herbal tea next to me and think sincerely and unconditionally: This is all great! What an interesting life I'm living!

I feel so incredibly grateful to have this comprehension of my efforts. It honours the hard work that everyone around me put into making these things exist – and it honours me, too. Because of my sobriety, I went back to aviation school and passed my check-ride, earning my private pilot's certificate. I could never have achieved this while still drinking. I also went back to the island of St Croix, this time sober. I went to AA meetings there in the old Moravian Church, at 8.30 am every day. I helped take care of my previous holiday hook-up, who had recently been in a bad accident, not driving a car but bike-riding drunk and breaking his back. He suffered third-degree burns when he was pinned under the engine of the truck he hit. As I performed chores for him and assisted in around-the-clock care, changing burn bandages and helping him to the bathroom and to shower, I started to think about moving to this island.

As I carved my sober path, a prayer started to resonate in my head, and years later it's still a mantra I find myself chanting sometimes when everything feels overwhelming.

God, let me be peaceful, calm and quiet in my head
Allow me not to be scared, sad and lonely,
Grant that I may seek to comfort than to be comforted
Understand than to be understood
Love than to be loved.

The words of the second half of this prayer are adapted from the infamous St Francis prayer. What I have come to notice is that, once upon a time, the self-effacing essence of asking to love than be loved would have echoed in my mind as me not deserving love. But that everyone else did. Now I understand the meaning of those words to be, 'I don't need to ask for love because I *am* love.' When this sense of complete acceptance and peace washes over me, as occasionally it does, it feels more blissful than any expensive glass of La Grande Dame champagne ever could.

chapter nine

A PLANE IS MORE COMFORTABLE THAN A BROOMSTICK

'Perfectly good aeroplanes
Goddesses Light and Dark
Kisses on my neck until it breaks
A love letter which bears my name
All the Good Things.'

N o matter what your physical age or what experiences you have had – you can transform your life. You can convert an attachment to loss and disappointment to an attitude of 'my cup is empty and I can fill it with anything!'

You can be useful and happy in the world.

Now it's time to walk the Witchy talk. Can I really fly? Yes – in a plane. Looking back, my move to the Caribbean and the reinvention of my life was an act of transformation that, if I had known what I would do ahead of time, I would have said was impossible! The last thing I did before leaving Los Angeles was pass my private pilot's check-ride and get a tattoo of a 1934 Boeing-Stearman propeller on my left forearm. The next day I was on a plane to relocate to the Caribbean. And this is when I started to experience the magic of operating flying machines and succeeding in the practical, mechanistic world of piloting and business aviation.

I wanted to forge an authentic, grounded life on my new island home, St Croix, in the U.S. Virgin Island, so I pestered a company called, Bohlke International Airways, for a job. They are a full-service Fixed Based Operator (FBO) and charter operator (like an airport terminal for private and general aviation).

Every day I would show up there at the office and ask if there was anything I could do. Finally, after three weeks of this, the general manager said to me, 'Well, what would you do?' I looked around the disorganised lobby and pointed at a large, ugly, glass shelving cabinet filled with old aviation maps and dust, and said, 'I would turn that into a gift store.'

He nodded and said, 'Have at it.'

So I went and bought local hot sauce, and had my girlfriend make some chaney and sea-glass necklaces, and I found a local lady who made soaps from locally harvested herbs and coconut oil. I cleaned out the glass cabinet, displayed everything prettily and made labels and description leaflets. I ran it all as a cash store … and all the products sold out in one week. After running it profitably for six weeks I was offered a full-time job as the company's marketing manager and charter-sales assistant. I took that same 'polish and improve' attitude and rebranded the company to the point where we became the Number One FBO in the Caribbean the second year I was there.

After being a rock star and the world's favourite Witch for a quarter of a century, I willingly entered corporate life when this family of aviators gave me a job. I knuckled down and over achieved for three years, growing from a person knowing relatively nothing to becoming a positive presence in the US national business aviation industry, attending giant trade shows, holding press conferences and putting this little family-run FBO on the international map. I made sure to parlay my marketing work into successful campaigns to benefit local youth, launching an aviation scholarship and other outreach programs to help young people forge careers in aviation – especially the girls.

I also had some funny brushes with celebrities, which brought back memories of my old life. It was late one Friday night in December and I was in the catering kitchen cutting up organic carrots for Lady Joan Branson to dip into her organic hummus, on a flight we were providing her the next day. The world's elite come to visit the Caribbean in season, and Sir Richard Branson and his wife frequently booked our jet. So did Paul McCartney, Mick Jagger, Kate Moss, Mark Zuckerberg … we were a popular, safe, private carrier in the region.

As I chopped the carrots I thought back to a time when I was a famous, Australian rock star, Witch and TV personality, and Richard (he wasn't a Sir back in November 1999) had invited me and my room mate bestie, *Neighbours* soap star Krista Vendy, onto the maiden flight of his Virgin Blue service in Australia. Also onboard was my girlfriend Natalie Imbruglia, sportsman Grant Kenny, and singer Deni Hines.

We flew with Richard from Melbourne to Sydney to Brisbane, spending the entire day with him on his big 737 and enjoying a party at a huge nightclub in Brisbane at the end of the day.

Richard asked me to cast a good spell on his airline as Natalie christened the plane by spraying champagne on the nose and the press took photos – it was a massively publicised event.

He is such a nice, funny, friendly man – so I did. I laid my hand on his plane and conjured an incantation for blessings of safety and good fortune for his new business.

All these years later, as I stood chopping carrots for his wife, it occurred to me that maybe the next day when I saw him I should tell him that I am the Witch who helped christen his airline all those years ago and clearly my good spell had worked!

But I decided not to. I was trying to start a quiet new life – and what would it achieve, anyway? Probably just confuse him! The leap from being a famous Australian rock star Witch to a marketing manager chopping up carrots in a little Caribbean airport kitchen might just seem too weird.

But it wasn't weird to me – this humble undertaking to start at the very bottom and rebuild my life from scratch was essential. So I didn't tell Richard – but I was the attendant on his wife's flight the next day and she loved the hummus and the carrots!

That was the last time I did the catering – after three years working hard for the Bohlke family I resigned on good terms and at the top of my game. I had saved almost every cent I earned and was ready to go to flight school to become a professional pilot.

It was when I identified that I wanted to fly so that I could contribute usefully to the world – be able to fly medical supplies, food and aid into remote, stricken regions – that a switch turned on inside my head and all of a sudden I could grasp and apply all the technical information. In 2016, three years after becoming a private pilot, I achieved my commercial, instrument and multi-engine certificate and ratings. In becoming a professional pilot I overcame my life-long, deep-seated conviction that I could be good but never good enough. Every time I get in a plane and fly it I feel quietly good. I have finally impressed myself enough to silence that cruel, belittling voice in my head. Of course it still sometimes resonates if I'm tired, lonely or hungry – especially in those dark hours at 3 am. No matter how Zen you are, shit can still get stressful … especially when you are on a mission to become a commercial pilot.

All last year during flight school I struggled to fall asleep and then stay asleep. My brain was wired all the time. I also experienced the most insane pain during the last weeks of my Commercial VFR school and checkride. My skin, my joints … everything was burning and aching. But somehow, in the midst of all the pain, and setback after setback, bad weather, citizenship issues, lack of money, I finally did the checkride and passed, achieving my Commercial VFR ticket on the '16Right' runway of Van Nuys Airport. It was bittersweet because when Jeff loved me we would watch the wonderful movie *One Six Right* about that historical airport and its famed runway, and I would say to him, 'I dream of one day landing on 16Right.' I never thought back then that he would leave me, and that to find balance and have the end of our life together make sense I would become a commercial pilot landing on that runway four years later.

Jeff actually was an amazing source of support and help in my intense year of flight school. Two years after our break-up we forged a gentle friendship and kept in touch. He is a flight instructor and helped me complete important parts of the commercial training required – without his support I never would have achieved my goal. He told me he was proud of me. Despite all the terrible things that happened at the end of our relationship, I still love him and would do it all again in a heartbeat. But I would be the better version of me that I have come to know in sobriety. I take responsibility for my role in not handling myself better and more positively as I went through my crisis of identity that last year we were together. I don't blame him for stopping loving me – I didn't love me, so how could anyone else?

I am grateful to enjoy a good friendship with Jeff now. And very happy to make him proud. Last year I thanked him for all the good times and especially the bad times – because they made me what I am today and I feel the happiest and best version of me I've ever been in my life.

The day after passing the Commercial checkride I was on a commercial plane to New Orleans to appear as a featured Witch and presenter at HexFest. My bestie Sarah came along with me. I was taking handfuls of ibuprofen but my skin would not stop burning and my joints hurt so much I sometimes muffled screams as I walked.

Sarah took me out to dinner to congratulate me for passing my checkride. We were in this gorgeous little restaurant in the French Quarter, eating organic food, and I still could not quite fathom that I had passed in the midst of the insane stress and fear of failure.

After dinner we went for a walk down Bourbon St, and as we passed the brightly lit bars I also contemplated how once I could only have celebrated a momentous event like this by drinking alcohol, and would have stopped to prop up each bar, on an insatiable mission to have a great night by drinking a lot.

Sarah and I actually talked about going into a bar so she could have a drink, but neither of us was super motivated. And then suddenly a howling wind blew down the street, lifting our hair straight up in the air … and it started to POUR! Giant sheets of rain crashed down from the sky. We ran into the doorway of a store in a side street. The rain shot past us sideways as the wind shrieked. Crouched next to us were two cute gutter boys, cheap guitars shoved under their steampunk-leather and battered-canvas jackets. We were all screaming! And laughing!

The onslaught of rain and wind continued and we were drenched and having snatches of conversations with the boys as the words were whipped out of our mouths by the wind. Finally it lessened a little as the tornado-like storm cell shifted across the city. The boys asked us what we were planning to do next (which was flattering!). I had it in my head that I had become man repellent. Sarah has a tendency to think the same way (we were both battle-scarred from the lack of a good man in each of our lives). But on this night we just laughed and wished them a wonderful evening and, as the rain continued in spurts, we ran up the middle of Bourbon St looking at all the people huddling in the bars.

I ran out into the middle of the crossroads – the traditional place where the dead would meet, pacts would be made and banishing rituals cast to bury what you want to get rid of.

Sarah took a photo of me.

In the photo I am drenched in my black dress and I have the biggest smile on my face. I left my pain at those enchanted crossroads in the French Quarter just steps away from Priestess Miriam's Voodoo Temple. When I got back to the hotel I realised this and I said to Sarah, 'All my pain is gone!'

I luxuriated in being pain free in the following days. I stroked my skin, rolled around in my sheets, stuffed myself with sugary beignets while happily sitting on the hard metal seats at Café du Monde, walked without grimacing, and conducted my Witchcraft workshops for HexFest waving my arms around and just beaming in pain-free joy! When I look back I'm quite sure the crazy pain was emotional and stress-related due to the pressures of school and passing my check ride. I had two more checkrides after my Commercial VFR last year – my Instrument and my Multi-engine. But I never had pain like that again. I really do think the magick of the crossroads that rainy night in New Orleans healed me.

But just because I didn't have searing, burning pain throughout my body it didn't mean that there was no suffering during the rest of my training.

There came the day that I reached my last checkride; my Multi-engine. It was with a different school and a different examiner. It was late October.

All the pilots I knew had said, 'Oh the Multi is easy; it's the Instrument that is the hardest.' I had passed my Instrument in September. The checkride had been crazy hard, the flight portion delayed by terrible weather. But it had been with the same examiner as for my Commercial, four months before, so I was slightly less stressed.

Even though everyone was saying the Multi would be easy, I knew better than to rest on my laurels. I studied harder than ever. I poured every cent into flight school. I lived on cheese sandwiches and packet soup. I would walk into school and hand over the $200 that I'd managed to scrounge from fire dancing for tips or doing a tarot reading, and I would say, 'I've sold a kidney and found some money – I can keep going!' A friend also lent me $500 so that I could take the last checkride – that would dramatically improve my possibilities of getting a job in aviation and allow me to operate the humanitarian aid flights that were the underlying reason for putting myself through all of this.

The oral portion of the test went pretty well. It was long – I was asked questions about the systems of the aircraft and other operating considerations, for two-and-a-half hours. I had heard this examiner was tough, but my extra-hard study seemed to have paid off when he seemed pleased with me and said, 'All right, let's go to the plane.'

Remember I got into the habit of purposefully failing in school a million years ago so I wouldn't be picked on for being smart? I got used to failing everything or barely passing – eventually this seemed normal. As a result, being tested is my least favourite thing in the world. I am terrified of failure. I make myself sick with worry. But I had studied really hard and carefully flown with my instructors to master the skills in order to pass the flight portion. That being said, this checkride was one of the most traumatising experiences of my entire life.

The two-and-a-half hours spent in that plane with the examiner yelling at me and failing engines left and right (which I expected because it's part of the Practical Test Standards as required by the Federal Aviation Administration) still was completely debilitating. When I was instructed to land the plane a final time and taxi over to the ramp, I had no idea if I had passed.

As I shut the engines down the examiner yelled at me: 'Do you feel like you've been tested?'

I said, 'Yes sir, I do.'

And then he said, 'Okay, you can go inside and ring the bell.'

'Ring the bell' is flight-school talk for 'I had passed' and I could go into the main building and ring the bell on the wall, to let everyone know.

In a daze I walked into the building.

When I reached up, grabbed the rope and clanged a single 'Dong', a group of people around the front counter, who had looked worried when I initially walked in, all smiled and broke into applause. I stood there soaked in sweat, feeling like someone had dug a pit, pushed me into it and then proceeded to throw stones and piss on me for the last two-and-a-half hours.

I completed the necessary paperwork to get my certificate and left the building.

I drove a mile away from the flight school, pulled over and burst into tears. Something that should've felt like an amazing accomplishment felt like the absolute worst experience of my life. I sat there crying in the car, alone, flashes of rejection by my father and being unloved by Jeff went through my mind. I had done it! I was a commercial multi-engine pilot … and yet it still wasn't enough. I felt no sense of accomplishment. I just felt shattered.

I called my beloved girlfriend Beki and asked if I could come to her. I had planned to go back to the house I was staying in near the airport, owned by my good friend Mats, but he was away and I needed a hug.

I drove to Beki's, slowly, in the endless LA traffic. When I reached her home her dog Maxwell jumped in my lap, and she hugged me for two hours while I cried. Then she made me a cup of herbal tea. I realised I wasn't crying because I was a failure. I was releasing the insane stress and fear of the last year of flight school and the last five years of rebuilding my life after Jeff left. I cried because I wasn't celebrating with champagne – I was drinking herbal tea. Even though Jeff and I had broken up, he said he would take me out to celebrate. But just like the old days when we were together, he got a work flight and our plans were cancelled. I would be taking myself out to the movies that night.

But to illustrate how much I cultivate a positive face in social media (which may not necessarily reflect real events), later that night I wrote this Facebook post:

I PASSED TODAY!! MULTI-ENGINE CHECKRIDE COMPLETE. It has been an incredible journey to start this year as a private pilot and finish it as a commercial single and multi-engine instrument rated pilot with the goal of working full time as a pilot and volunteering humanitarian aid flying services.

Thank you to all my old and new friends who let me sleep on their couches and in their beds and let me eat food from their fridge this year, as I saved and scraped up every cent to pour into flight training – thank you to everyone who cheered me along as I struggled through fear of failure and not being good enough. This truly was the most challenging thing I have ever done in my adult life. I'm so grateful I could do you proud.

It's incredible to finally arrive at this moment. I leave Los Angeles back to the island's tomorrow.

To celebrate tonight I took myself on a date to see Sully – at the glamorous Sundance Cinema on Sunset Blvd – and enjoyed a gourmet ice cream sandwich and Ferrero Rocher chocolates. (Great movie – perfect for a post check ride celebration.)

I think I will be able to really sleep tonight for the first time in months. I'm so happy to be able to share this good news with you! Thank you again, everyone for coming on this journey with me!

Footnote: A female pilot called me a week later after seeing my Facebook post, to congratulate me. She asked, 'Was it easy?' I said no and told her about the 'thrown in a pit and being pissed on' analogy. She laughed and said, 'Well, I was going to tell you that the examiner you flew with made my big, strong, male friend cry in the cockpit on his checkride – at least you waited until you drove away.'

I took a small amount of solace in this.

Recently I had an emergency in a plane I was flying. The landing gear would not deploy. There were other mechanical issues presenting in the aircraft as I reached for the emergency checklist and calmly handled the situation, successfully deploying the gear and fixing the other problems.

My passengers and I landed safely.

Maybe some of that 'being calm in the face of chaos' experience of my multi-engine checkride paid off.

I continue to forge a new life. At the time of writing I have just completed my first mission to Haiti – I am honouring my promise to the God of my understanding, in doing this service work.

When I posted a report on my first aid mission (on social media) I had pilots asking me how to get involved with aid work. The first step, like anything in life, really, is *really wanting* it. I remember that's what someone told me when I got sober. 'You've got to want it.' This wisdom is in the chapter of AA's Big Book titled 'How it Works': 'If you have decided you *want* what we have and are ready to go to any lengths to get it, then you are ready to take certain steps.'

I really wanted it.

And I was lucky that someone referred me to a woman named Mandy Thody, director of the Good Samaritan Foundation of Haiti, who had been working in aid relief in Haiti for a number of years after the earthquake in 2010. She was on the island of Ile-a-Vache when Hurricane Matthew hit in 2016. Everything that the Foundation had built – the school, the farm, the gardens – was destroyed or severely damaged. Thankfully the well-built foundations of buildings erected by Mandy's team, stayed.

I then got even luckier. Turns out Mandy lives on the same island as me. When she returned from the hurricane strike, I was able to meet her in person and work on putting together the flights necessary to replenish what the community lost. We conducted two flights – the first delivering 350 laying chicks, 100 pounds of seed and feeder bunnies – to create a renewable protein source and help fulfil the 540 family meals and 270 school lunches the

Foundation is committed to providing to the community every day. The second flight followed up with school supplies, building materials and tools.

So how to get involved in Aid work? It takes asking around, being willing to work hard and trying again and again. I had so many rejections as I tried to identify and procure a plane. But I kept asking. And then I found a generous plane owner who said yes, they would donate their plane. Then there was tons of research to prepare for every outcome, tons of paperwork for customs, permits and handling, and a positive, patient attitude on the days of the flights.

I know some of the bigger aid-relief organisations employ pilots. I decided to work with grassroots operations and donate my time and skills – hoping to provide direct and immediate help to the communities and avoid the bottleneck that can occur with larger aid-relief organisations. Small steps can add up to big changes over time. I want to start small, learn as much as I can so that I am useful and not a liability, and keep identifying opportunities to be helpful.

I hope this is helpful info for those of you who want to be of service!

Selfishly, I love doing this charity work because it makes me feel good. It makes everyone feel good – the donators, the people implementing the mission, and the recipients of the charity.

Here in the islands there are vestiges of my former life in the entertainment industry – I am still entertaining people as I take them on scenic aerial tours. Various aviation magazines also now write articles about me (as it turns out), although I do not seek them out in a desperate attempt for approval and self-promotion. Far from it – the writers come to me and I do the stories hoping that I may inspire other girls to fly – especially girls my age. It's never too late in life to spread your wings and fly!

But as amazing as the last four sober years have been in rebirthing my life, I can still fall back into familiar patterns of attachment and pain, stress and overachieving. But I recognise them and can stop the ball rolling down the hill before it gets too large and obliterates me.

Like remembering the power of saying Yes.

Whilst writing this book I was in a major head funk in the streets of Old San Juan, unable to join my female pilot friends for dinner due to San Sebastián festival traffic. Traffic grid-locked, I got out of my Uber car and headed back to the house I was staying at (owned by my friends and right in the middle of Calle San Sebastián). My head was spinning with the stress of not completing things properly and I decided to go back to the desk and continue trawling through uncomfortable memories for this autobiography, as I had been all day (at the time, 40 000 words and counting).

I started to walk up a cobblestone alley toward home and my laptop … and I heard beautiful music. I turned around and followed my ears into the Plaza des Armas. There was a lone soprano saxophonist playing on a bench. The music was so soothing – it lifted my heart. I thought, Oh I should go home and work on the book. But instead I sat behind the player, on a park bench between two homeless men, and listened.

The music flowed over me as coloured lights bounced off the beautiful old buildings and trees. There was a team setting up a stage for the festival, at the edge of the square. But the square was quiet, except for the player's magical music. After one song, I thought, Oh I should be moving on back to work. And I wanted to leave a tip. I only had a $10 note. So I walked to a little cafe on the corner and bought a small pastry so I could walk back and give the player a tip. And he saw me and invited me to stay. I thought I should leave … but instead I said yes. He kept playing and I kept listening, my heart and head growing lighter. And then one of the homeless guys started singing, in Spanish, and he and the player jammed, and it was perfect. And then the player and I chatted a bit and I asked if I could fire dance.

I went home and got my fire tools and came back. And lit up. The homeless guy in yellow couldn't believe I came back. It was all totally spontaneous. Totally wonderful. A crowd of people gathered and the player and I jammed – fire and sax. And then a lovely couple appeared and danced a sensual tango. It was a magickal night borne out of saying yes for the joy of the moment. I felt so happy and blessed to have a new friend in Frank – the travelling musician, and the homeless Angel of the streets, in the yellow shirt, who hugged us all to his chest that night and said, 'Life is for living now! That's what it's all about!'

chapter ten

50 DOES NOT SUCK

'Got the sun in my face
I gotta keep moving
Let the shadows fall behind me ...'

F ifty really doesn't suck. Well, it doesn't have to – it depends how you live it. I am a sober, yoga-practising, mindful-thinking, useful contributor to the planet … Well, that's what I aim to be, one day at a time.

This makes me happy. My body is healthy and is fun to inhabit. My mind is mostly peaceful. I know how to look 'younger': I smile – an instant, natural facelift.

In our society 50 once demarcated the time when a woman is no longer sexually desirable. Now we continue to live longer, as a species, and there are catchphrases like '50 is the new 30' being flung about with relish.

It all relates back to our desirability – our 'mate worthiness'. I can go through spiraling descents into insecurity and emotional exhaustion over the five years since Jeff … if I allow myself to focus only on the fact that I have had no meaningful, lasting connection with a man – only brief, painful ones.

What is the starlight shining in this dark sky of contemplation?

When an interaction becomes toxic I recognise the danger signs and get out fast, rather than stick around and try to change (aka 'fix') the man to what I think he could/should be. Or, more ominously, try to change myself to fit what he thinks I should be.

This is very good. I have come a long way. I can feel grateful rather than resentful.

I only have myself to blame for the hell inside my head (if it happens to be raging).

I'm sharing this with you in the hope that it will encourage you not to give up if you share a similar struggle. Recognise destructive thoughts and impulses to sabotage yourself and gracefully let them go. And when it all gets too hard, stop obsessing about yourself and do something to help others. It breaks the self-destruct cycle every time.

Recently I had a difficult month of constant depression. It was like I had been injected with a drug called 'Grief and Despair', but I kept going. Getting out of bed, teaching yoga, fire dancing, being a positive ray of light to everyone I crossed paths with, 'faking happiness' until I hopefully felt it for real.

One evening I was massively weary and contemplating the endless onslaught of shit inflicted on me, and conjured by me … and suddenly, like in the early AA days, I had a 'God Shot' and a voice in my head spoke to me. It said, 'Fiona, I cannot protect you from all the shitty people and awful things in the world, but I promise you, when you are going through hard stuff I am going to put Angels around you and they will help you.'

And suddenly my perspective shifted and I realised that during all these terrible times there had been amazing, wonderful people helping me through.

I could feel grateful for all the rotten shit going on because it gave me an opportunity to connect with beautiful, helpful people and be grateful for all the happier turns of events when they eventually came – because they always do if you let them.

It's true – Angels are always around you if you take the time to look up and notice them. Sometimes the hardest thing to do is to be humble enough to accept help.

So, as I get not older, but better at living, I again think about a life partner. It would be a distraction. A 'love of my life' would take up all my time. How would I have a full-time job and have time to organise charity flights, youth outreach, etc. etc. etc?

If I was in love with a guy I would just want to lie on the couch and cuddle and eat yummy food and have sex.

Haha! Maybe one day. Maybe never. I'm grateful that I've learned that wonderful, fulfilling, peaceful love comes from many sources – including myself. I can be my own significant 'other'.

If a 'perfect match', 'life partner', 'husband' or 'soul mate' are mere concepts marketed to us to make marriage appealing and to make women conveniently malleable to fit into conventional Western society, then, as a closet anarchist, I am prepared to never have 'it' happen!

I am open to multiple experiences with different humans, learning and growing for a time together and then moving on.

I've turned away from the contrived notions of 'my best years are behind me' and 'wine is the solution' (I cringe when I see framed pictures of that saying displayed in trendy gift stores).

I have learned to live a more youthful, adventurous life than ever.

It was very liberating and en*light*ening to let go of most of my personal possessions and strip away everything I own down to three bags, when I moved to the islands.

However, there are nine boxes of Def FX and Witch 'fame' memorabilia in my girlfriend's garage in Bakersfield. I was throwing it all out and coming across some fun items like Def FX's Smashing Pumpkins 1996 Tour booklet and a poster of the Australian cover of *Playboy*. I posted pics on Facebook and was immediately accosted by multiple messages including one from my friend, a professional archivist named Louise Trott, who said I must not throw out the memorabilia – that it has a place in Australian archival records. She pointed out that I had a significant role as a ground-breaking woman in the Australian music scene and that my memorabilia is of historical importance. She also, emphasised that I am probably Australia's best-known Witch! And that makes me a unique character in Australian culture.

I did what she told me and kept some stuff – some of it has been reproduced in this book! I let go of a lot of it too.

· O.

During the writing of this book I hoped that it would be good for its readers, but at times, as I trawled through painful memories, I wondered why the hell I was doing it!

The opportunity came to me out of the blue from a previous publisher of mine – their creative team contacted me through Facebook and asked if I had another book in me. After this lovely surprise and a lot of 'good faith' writing by me (i.e. no money on the table,) the project was dropped. The money guys at the company said it wouldn't sell in 'the minimum corporate mandate' because I wasn't famous enough and/or on TV anymore. This was quite a blow and I wasn't sure what to do. This opportunity had come to me – I hadn't asked for it. I just wanted to be an anonymous pilot flying in the Caribbean for the second half of my life.

I decided the right thing to do would be to share with other publishers what I had written – to honour the work. And the wonderful Lisa Hanrahan at Rockpool gave me the opportunity to be published by her. I arrived exactly where I am meant to be.

Again, I hope that this book has helped you … because writing it has helped me, as it turns out. In recalling my life it has given me the perspective to see that I have learned to nourish and nurture myself – instead of tear myself apart.

I don't have to suffer quite so much to take a few steps forward in life.

It's a beautiful, relaxing feeling. At 50 I am letting my life be an enlightened, conscious practice in acceptance of personal happiness. I think that's better than the way I lived before.

Don't get older, get better!

There's nothing special about me – I'm not extra strong.

I'm not extra gifted. One thing I *am*, is persistent. I just can't give up. I encourage you to never give up. Every single step you take in a better direction adds up to big, positive changes over time. And you arrive at the best version of yourself.

There are some things I consider important to a happy and healthy life. Here's what helps me every day:

Solitude

Solitude no longer means cutting myself off from people in a familiar pursuit of feeling sad and abandoned. I don't confuse it with loneliness. Solitude is uplifting, restorative, joyful.

I can be in a plaza full of people in Old San Juan and feel solitude. I love being the eye of the storm – standing in peace as the world whirls around me.

I find the best way to experience solitude as a healing, nourishing force is to be in Nature. Nature is the best therapy. I make sure I take a quiet moment to put my bare feet on the bare earth every day.

Signs

As I write this the rains of the past few weeks have finally stopped and the morning has dawned bright and clear. It's a beautiful reminder that no matter how stormy and crazy life can get, there will always come the moment when clarity and peace reign supreme. I pay attention to signs; I trust them.

Yesterday I had come to the end of a very busy day and I was sitting at Frederiksted Pier catching my breath and watching the last moment of the sunset … and feeling overwhelmed with the many tasks I had committed to: write a new book for my publisher, practice with Def FX for our 20-year reunion tour, write a new song for DEF FX, build my flight hours as quickly as possible so I can get a full-time job as a pilot, teach yoga, execute and fly the humanitarian aid flight I had committed to, find time to eat, sleep and also, just maybe, have a moment to relax and keep up my freediving and breath-holding skills in the ocean. I felt so overwhelmed it was paralysing and I didn't know what to do. Something on the concrete to my left caught my attention. I walked over and saw this drawn in chalk … and I knew what to do.

Signs are everywhere if we are open to them. As long as we pay attention to them and stay out of our own way, everything can work out great.

Wealth

I'm not talking about money! I have very little of it, but an enormous wealth of friends and good people in my life. I really live by the adage of 'paying it forward'. I like to connect people with people, and people with opportunities.

Rather than fullness in my pocket I feel fullness in my heart when I help someone. I hope the groundwork I have laid in my life, the experiences I've had, as well as lessons I've learned, may benefit others in some way.

I experience great satisfaction in seeing someone prosper – or just smile – from my help. Or, in the case of my readings, hear the relief in someone's voice when an emotional block they have been suffering from is released, thanks to my guidance. At times I have helped others at the expense of my own wellbeing, however. I own my choice, but I have learned that I can't help others if my own arm is broken. There's a difference between being helpful and being an enabling people pleaser!

Wealth for me is now measured by the quality of life enjoyed with peace of mind, acceptance and by being surrounded by positive people and experiences – in that I am rich indeed.

Girlfriends

My girlfriends are my lifeline. At times of joy and of pain they have been there. I really cultivate and treasure my friendships with the special girls in my life – and there's no age discrimination! My island BFF is eight-year-old Haley!

There's also no species discrimination! My best animal girlfriend is my dog Fifi. Two years ago she came running out of the Crucian rainforest with a chewed-through leash hanging off her neck and bones poking through her skin … and rescued me. I love her so much it hurts. I am so proud of her and so grateful for her finding me.

Friendships are the elixir of life.

Yoga

Yoga is the foundation of my life now. I have always practised a little yoga over the years, but never in a devout and disciplined way. Until I moved to St Croix, which has a small, wonderful yoga

Top: I love practising
yoga all over the world -
I take my travel mat with
me everywhere - here in
Dubai in 2016.

Bottom: Fire is delicious!

community, and I was blessed to practise under the guidance of Laura Hunter Kaough – an amazing yogini and soul, who I can now also call a dear friend. When her husband's job took their family away from St Croix, after four years of being her student, I started teaching her classes. I love the privilege and pleasure of sharing my practice and helping others grow in theirs. We create our flow together – I am grateful for the amazing students I have.

Yoga is the key to living a flexible, energised life – physically mentally and spiritually. I take my mat everywhere with me.

Dancing

There's a saying: 'Dance like no one is watching.' I seem to end up dancing when everyone *is* watching. The important thing is to dance every day, no matter what. I consider yoga a form of dancing, especially when I move through the Dancing Warrior sequence in a Vinyasa Flow. Daily dancing – moving your body in a joyful way – is key to celebrating your existence.

When I arrived on St Croix, I went to a workshop held by a local fire-dancing troupe. The founder, Kiki, became a dear girlfriend. But in those early days I just kept showing up at their gigs, asking if there was anything I could do. I helped with fire safety; I lugged gear. I bought my own poi and I started practising – hitting myself over the head, night after night, as I stood in the kitchen of the old building I lived in, with its high ceilings and centipedes running around my feet.

Nothing could distract me from practising.

After joining the troupe practice sessions a number of times, I could participate in a show. And then another and another, until a year later I was a lead dancer. I expanded my repertoire to include different props and skills, fans, torches, palms, wands and fire eating. The biggest step was getting confident and comfortable enough with fire (and yes, you get burned a lot, especially in the early days) that I could pour my entertainer's personality, uninhibited, into dancing with fire. Just like I would do on stage with Def FX – I rocked out with fire dancing. It turned out to be a crowd-pleasing combination.

I started fire dancing at the age of 47. Years after being told I needed knee reconstruction and had a damaged sacrum (blah blah – doctors love to tell you what's wrong with you) I now focus on what's right when it comes to physical things, and doing what makes me feel good. To be able to keep dancing daily, I have little rituals. When I'm walking up and down stairs or hills, instead of focusing on how crunchy and painful my knees are, I reinforce and thank them by saying in my mind 'My beautiful, strong, steady knees, I love how you carry me up and down these stairs with such ease.' I draw my stomach in and imagine I have a magickal cord at the top of my head, pulling me upwards and taking the weight out of my knees. I reinforce and celebrate the gift of my body in motion.

From a magickal perspective, having fire carve an arc around your body and burn through your aura is very cleansing and cathartic, too – it keeps me in good spiritual health.

Adventures

I make sure I have adventures every day as well as plan future ones: Big and small. Having done so many things I am often asked what future adventures I am conjuring.

Despite living in the Caribbean, I have a dream to go to the Maldives – on a beautiful holiday … or work there flying seaplanes for resort guests.

At some point in my life I would also like to disappear into Mongolia with just a backpack and a yak-wool coat.

I would love to practise yoga in India.

I would love to walk the Camino de Santiago and visit my girlfriend who lives in a Witches' forest in Spain.

I'd like to go back to Africa and explore more of that extraordinary continent.

And snowboard in Switzerland. My last big fear is snow! I'm terrified of slipping and screwing up. But I have a Swiss friend who says he'll teach me, so one day I'm going to do it!

As I think about my future plans, they all involve travel – further and outward, away from where I started. I will always be an explorer.

If there ever came a day I would be relieved of wanderlust, my girlfriend Sarah and I have promised each other that, if we are both single at 70, we will create a commune together at her parents' farm in New Mexico. She loves driving and I can fly us in and out of there, so we can go and explore places together by road and air when we need a break from hiding away from the world.

Sarah is a wonderful singer and songwriter, so she can make music and I will fire dance to it. And we can do fun Witchy shamanic rituals and yoga out on the plains amongst the volcanic rocks.

Living in the Moment

My girlfriend Laura invited me to her home for impromptu drinks this evening. She enjoyed her Apothic Red Wine and I enjoyed the organic passionfruit juice and soda she made me as I decompressed.

I had just spent three hours with federal agents, looking at video of a shooting that had happened in front of where I have lived during writing the last chapters of this book. A drunken brawl over a girl turned into three attempts of murder and was captured by my house's video cameras, which were aimed at the street.

I felt like I was in an episode of *NCIS* or *Law and Order* as I watched the Feds getting excited by what the video had captured and talking in cop-speak about how this could be used as evidence and how it matched and validated sporadic witness accounts and highlighted the actions of nefarious people who had withheld information when interviewed.

This scenario reminded me that I live in a bit of a bubble: I don't watch the news, I don't gossip about all the terrible things going on in the world. I like my bubble, which is focused on what is good and what is going well in human life.

When Laura texted me as the Feds were leaving and invited me down the road to her peaceful home filled with magnificent art, sculptures and plants, it felt like an affirmation of my choice to not buy into the media-fueled negative drama and fear that is encouraged in our existence.

I love spending time with Laura. She is very compassionate and, as the evening went on, I told her I was emotionally tired, struggling a bit with depression and had identified it was because I did not have a companion in my life. I also told her I was consciously trying to view my feelings rationally and analytically. See it for what it is. See all the great reasons to not have a boyfriend and acknowledge why it feels like something is missing.

I would like someone to care where I am at the end of the day. I would like a guy to enjoy me, go on adventures with me, hug me, love me.

Because we are new friends, Laura asked me a lot of animated questions about my life. As I answered her I contemplated yet again what an unusual life I have lived.

I feel like I have to keep proving myself and working it out. What am I? How can I earn the space I am taking on the planet?

That's when Laura said something beautiful and really helpful to me in that moment:

'Maybe our reason for living doesn't have to be tangible. We don't need to have a definition. We just accept that we are *this*. We are okay with it.'

Laura Daen is a muse – her husband was celebrated sculptor, Lindsay Daen. He died of natural causes sixteen years ago. Laura is now the custodian of his art, his amazing sculptures. That morning she had also been thinking about relationships and the quality a companion can brings to one's life. We both feel ready to be in love.

In the meantime, I will keep on with my life and focusing on being useful in the world. I can be okay with the weird person that I am.

My reason for living doesn't have to be tangible or defined. It just is.

The Glamorous Life of a Pilot of the Caribbean.

Today was a long day of flying cargo, people and animals around, with terribly achy legs, pounding head and my period due (nothing like having to step hard on the right rudder in a strong crosswind with two × 300 horsepower engines roaring in your ears, when you're premenstrual!).

Finally, I was home and could get out of my sweat-drenched uniform and put on something comfortable.

I went for a walk to the ancient Spanish Fort, El Morro, which bounds the seaside neighbourhood of Old San Juan.

I just went to sit quietly and watch the sunset.

Alone. Again. Naturally.

But I wasn't alone. The wind whooshed past my ears in airy strokes, wrapping around my body, before plunging over the cliff and spilling across the swells of waves, leaving foamy trails in its wake. The surging green-grey sea massaged my eyes; great ribbons and sheets of water eased my mind and distracted me from my pain. The ancient stone foundations beneath me were warm from a day spent sunbaking under the bright Caribbean sky. I was alone – but hugged by life. In the centre of everything, life wrapped itself around me and, as I sat there, undefined and hugged by life, I felt great peace.

THANK YOU

Elmarie and Otto Wypkema, my dear friends, it all started in South Africa with you and Mjejane! Thank you for launching me on this written adventure … and taking me flying in your beautiful helicopter!

Carol and Owen Johnson – my beloved island parents, thank you for believing in me and opening your home and hearts to me … and my pup, Fifi!

Kim Damratowski and Roland Manarin – who would have thought a chance meeting at an air rally would set us off on this journey of friendship? I am forever grateful for your support.

My long-time girlfriends … my lifelines … Sarah Lassez, Beki Colada, Dannii Minogue – I am blessed by our decades of friendship – thank you for guiding me and blowing the wind in my sails when you knew I couldn't. Thank you for your unconditional love.

All the magnificent Goddesses in my life, I am so grateful to know you and love you … Georgia Cassimatis, Laura Hunter Kaough, Shelleylyn Brandler, Devin Devasquez, Sara Ell, Melissa Woodbridge, Sharilea Hitchcock, Rachel Nicole von Kaenel, Kamala Mathis, Peggy Partida, Kim Webster, Laura Daen, Ethlie Ann Vare, Mandy Thody, Emma Lynch, Lejla Cas, Kiki Mason, Louise Trott, Fiona Wight, Wendy Hannam and Lydia Visintin.

My brothers in rock – Ant Banister, Marty Basha and Blake Gardner.

My big sisters in aviation – Magali Lewis, CJ Freeman and Lindsey Floyd.

My best boy friend in Los Angeles – Mats Holmberg.

My best boy friend in Australia – Robert Wilmshurst.

My favourite Witches in the World – Christian Day and Brian Cain.

My Facebook Family, Instagram Family and my Def FX Family – I love how close we are in energy, no matter where we are on the planet!

All the amazing, magickal people I have crossed paths with, whether in person, through my written word or in song, and who welcome my presence into their space – I am so grateful and happy to be sharing this wild adventure of a life with you!

'All Them Witches' for providing the soundtrack to the writing of this book! You are my favourite band!

To the legendary literary ladies I am lucky to know … without you this book wouldn't have happened! Claudia Boutote, Alison Urquhart, Jane Palfreyman, Judika Illes and Roberta Ivers.

And last, but not least, my heartfelt thanks to Team Rockpool – how completely blessed am I to be doing this with such awesome people?!

Lisa Hanrahan, you are not only my publisher now, but a dear and trusted friend – YOU are the Rockstar! Paul Dennett, Andrés Engracia, you created the best tag #FionaHorneIsBackBitches – haha!! And my girl, Jessica Le, thank you for going above and beyond on the homestretch!

My editor, Katie Evans – thank you for always encouraging me, never scaring me and helping me find the words … and then cutting them ever so kindly!

One final thank you … to YOU for reading this book!

Join me on my adventures!
www.fionahorne.com